PRESIDENTIAL COINCIDENCES,

AMAZING FACTS

AND

COLLECTIBLES

BY

LAURENCE L. COOK

Copyright © 2013

All rights reserved. No part of this book may be reproduced in
any form or by electronic or mechanical means including
information storage and retrieval systems without permission
in writing from the author, except by a reviewer,
who may quote brief passages in a review.

Published by:
Nick Of Time Printing
2937 Memorial Highway
Dallas, Pennsylvania 18612
www.nickoftimeprinting.com

Photographs by: Linda Cook

Printed and bound in the United States of America.

ISBN 978-1-4675-6463-2

DEDICATION

I dedicate this book to Diane, my first lady.

ACKNOWLEDGMENTS

I would like to thank and acknowledge the following people:
My parents, Larry and Joyce Cook for teaching me to respect our leaders
and encouraging my interest in presidential history at an early age.
My sister, Linda for her expert photography skills.
My wife, Diane for her help in turning my manuscript into a book.
Joe Antonishak and John Phillips for all of their help in finding great
pieces of presidential memorabilia to add to my collection.
And also, President Jimmy Carter and Rosalynn Carter
for their inspiration and encouragement.

CONTENTS

INTRODUCTION 5

CHAPTER 1 - HISTORY REPEATS 6

CHAPTER 2 - THE DEATH OF A PRESIDENT 8

CHAPTER 3 - ROAD TO THE WHITE HOUSE 10

CHAPTER 4 - NAMES 13

CHAPTER 5 - FUTURE PRESIDENTS SERVING SITTING PRESIDENTS 16

CHAPTER 6 - PRESIDENTIAL INSPIRATION 19

CHAPTER 7 - RELATIVES AND RELATIONSHIPS 21

CHAPTER 8 - WASHINGTON TO OBAMA 23

CHAPTER 9 - COLLECTIBLES 31

CONCLUSION 101

BIBLIOGRAPHY 102

INTRODUCTION

Since 1789, Americans have been intrigued with the office of the president. Not just the president himself captures one's fascination and marks a spot in history, but so does his family, staff, acquaintances and the events that occur during his term (s) and his lifetime.

Throughout presidential history a close look at the office, the president and the people that surround him reveal many interesting, and sometimes almost unbelievable happenings that interlock one administration to another. For example, most of us have read about the similarities of Abraham Lincoln and John F. Kennedy. They will again be mentioned in this book. However, many more presidential coincidences, oddities and unique relationships pertain to other members of this elite group we address as "Mr. President".

As one who since childhood has been intrigued by these interesting and even strange facts, I found that a great way to study the presidency was to collect related memorabilia. Researching newly acquired memorabilia leads to the discovery of more and more facts. Learning more facts continues the quest for more memorabilia. After several years, I ended up with two historical collections, one of facts and one of memorabilia.

This book is designed to share both collections under one cover. The intention of this book is to inspire.

CHAPTER 1

HISTORY REPEATS

IMPEACHMENT

In 1868, Andrew Johnson faced impeachment resulting from charges that he violated the Tenure of Office Act when he dismissed Secretary of War Edwin Stanton. In 1998, William Jefferson Clinton faced impeachment resulting from charges of perjury while under investigation for the Monica Lewinsky scandal.

The Senate exonerated both men when their respective votes fell short of the two-thirds majority needed for conviction, allowing them to remain in office. Both men successfully came through their respective scandals and will be more easily remembered in history because of the unusual and unlikely event of impeachment.

These two very different men; one a rough and sometimes rogue president entrenched in the mid-19th century post civil war era, the other a well polished and soft spoken late 20th century chief executive couldn't be more different. However, on one specific day in each of these men's term of service they were close to being identical. This day is the day that each of these men awaited the results of the Senate vote on their particular impeachment proceedings. One can only imagine that both men must have gone through the same thoughts, hopes, fears and prayers while awaiting his fate. One can be certain that both men felt exactly the same feeling of exhilaration and relief upon receiving news of the Senate vote. Two men forever locked in history by a constitutional process.

LIKE FATHER...

John Adams was the second president, but the first to see his son John Quincy Adams attain the same office. One hundred and seventy five years later, former President George H. W. Bush witnessed his son George W. Bush taking the presidential oath.

Both of these presidential offspring that were destined to become president shared the same first name of their father but a different middle name.

TAKE TWO

One president repeated history for himself. In 1885 Grover Cleveland became the twenty-second president of the United States. However, in 1888, despite winning the majority of the popular vote, Cleveland lost the electoral vote allowing Benjamin Harrison, grandson of former President William Henry Harrison to become the twenty-third president. In 1892, Cleveland again ran against Harrison. Cleveland won the election and became the twenty-fourth president. This made him the only president to be re-elected after leaving office.

SHARING A BIRTHDAY

James K. Polk was born on November 2, 1795. Exactly seventy years later on November 2, 1865 Warren Harding was born.

NOBEL PEACE PRIZE

Four presidents have received The Nobel Peace Prize. Theodore Roosevelt, Woodrow Wilson, Jimmy Carter and Barack Obama.

GRAMMY AWARD

Three presidents have won a Grammy Award. Jimmy Carter, Bill Clinton and Barack Obama have all won for Best Spoken Word Album.

CHAPTER 2

THE DEATH OF A PRESIDENT

A NATION MOURNS

Eight presidents have died while in office. In 1841 William Henry Harrison was the first to die in office, followed by Zachary Taylor in 1850. Abraham Lincoln died in 1865, the first to be assassinated. In 1881, James Garfield fell victim to an assassin, as did William McKinley in 1901. Warren G. Harding, a president in midst of scandal, died in 1923, and Franklin Delano Roosevelt passed away suddenly in 1945 while having an official presidential portrait done in Warm Springs, Georgia. The last president to die in office was John F. Kennedy in 1963, the fourth president to succumb to the act of an assassin.

The first two presidents to die in office, William Henry Harrison and Zachary Taylor, both died in the White House while under the care of the same physician, Dr. Thomas Miller.

LINCOLN and KENNEDY

Of the eight presidents that have died while in office, a look at Abraham Lincoln and John F. Kennedy reveal many coincidences. On their political climb toward the presidency, both served in the U.S. House of Representatives. Lincoln was elected to the House in 1846. Kennedy was elected to the House in 1946. Lincoln was elected president in 1860; Kennedy was elected president in 1960. Both men were assassinated on a Friday and each was sitting next to his wife at the time. A vice president with the last name of Johnson succeeded both men. Both assassins John Wilkes Booth and Lee Harvey Oswald were killed before they could be brought to trial. Abraham Lincoln was assassinated in a theater. Kennedy's assassin was captured in a theater.

COOLIDGE

At the time of his death on January 5, 1933, former President Calvin Coolidge was working on a jigsaw puzzle of George Washington.

JULY 4TH

John Adams, the second president and Thomas Jefferson, the third president both died on the exact same day. These men passed on July 4, 1826, the nation's fiftieth birthday. Close friends early in their careers, John Adams and Thomas Jefferson grew distant throughout the years due to political differences. However, John Adams last words were "Thomas Jefferson survives." Ironically Adams was not aware that Thomas Jefferson had died earlier in the day.

On July 4, 1831, James Monroe, the fifth president became the third president to die on America's birthday.

Nearly in keeping with his two predecessors and his immediate successor James Madison, the fourth president came very close to dying on America's birthday. In June 1836, it became apparent that the ailing past president would die very soon. His physician offered up the idea to medicate him until July 4th so that he would die on Independence Day like Adams, Jefferson and Monroe. Madison refused his doctor's idea and passed away on June 28th.

Although there were three presidents that died on July 4th, another president met deadly fate on that day. Zachary Taylor, the twelfth U.S. president became ill on July 4, 1850 after attending ceremonies at the Washington Monument. It is reported in historical accounts that he developed severe stomach upset after drinking ice water, drinking milk and eating cherries at the ceremonies. Five days later on July 9, 1850, he died in the White House.

INAUGURATION HAZARD

In 1841, while delivering the longest inaugural speech in history, William Henry Harrison developed a cold that later turned into pneumonia and took his life.

In 1853, while attending Franklin Pierce's inauguration, Millard Fillmore's wife Abigal came down with a cold, which developed, into pneumonia, killing her less than a month after she ceased being First Lady.

GARFIELD and McKINLEY

James Garfield and William McKinley both fought in the Civil War and came through it unscathed, only to be shot and killed while in office. Neither one of these wounded presidents died immediately from their wounds. President Garfield lived for eleven weeks after being shot and President McKinley lived for eight days. Both presidents died in the month of September.

CHAPTER 3

ROAD TO THE WHITE HOUSE

RAPID SUCCESSION

Of the 44 U.S. presidents, a significant percentage of them made it to the White House by succession rather than election. Had it not been for unfortunate happenings to their predecessors, nine men may never have become president. The following vice presidents became president because of the untimely death of an incumbent president: John Tyler 1841, Millard Fillmore 1850, Andrew Johnson 1865, Chester Arthur 1881, Theodore Roosevelt 1901, Calvin Coolidge 1923, Harry Truman 1945, and Lyndon Johnson 1963.

In 1974 Gerald Ford became president upon the resignation of Richard Nixon.

FRANKLIN and THEODORE

Along with having the same last name, Franklin Roosevelt took virtually the same trail to the White House as Theodore Roosevelt did several years before.

Both men were born to prominent New York State families. Both attended Harvard and Columbia Law School. Theodore became very active in New York State politics and became a leader in the Republican Party there. Franklin also became very active in New York State politics and became a leader in the Democratic Party. Theodore served as assistant secretary of the navy in the McKinley administration; Franklin served as assistant secretary of the navy under Woodrow Wilson. In 1898, Theodore was elected governor of New York. In 1928, Franklin was elected governor of New York. Theodore served as vice president under McKinley. Franklin was nominated for vice president on the Democratic ticket in 1920, but was defeated by Republicans Harding and Coolidge. Theodore became president in 1901. Thirty-two years later Franklin became the second President Roosevelt.

ARMED SERVICES

Many presidents served in military service. For many of those, their participation and leadership in historical military events shone a spotlight on them that glanced a reflection toward the presidency.

George Washington served as Commander In Chief of the Continental Army for the Revolutionary War, leading America to independence.

America's seventh president, Andrew Jackson, fought in the Revolutionary War at a young age but his fame arose as a major general in the War of 1812. His military leadership brought victories against Indians and the British, including the famous battle of New Orleans. The victories thrust him into hero status on a national level. William Henry Harrison was also a major general in the War of 1812, winning the Battle of the Thames in Canada. In 1841, he became the ninth president.

Prior to becoming president, Zachary Taylor had a distinguished 40-year military career including serving in the War of 1812. Known as: "Old Rough and Ready", he also gained national recognition as a hero in the Mexican War. Four years later, he was elected president, his first political office.

Franklin Pierce also gained some notoriety from the Mexican War. When the war broke out, he enlisted and quickly rose to the rank of brigadier general despite seeing very little combat.

Like Zachary Taylor and Franklin Pierce, Ulysses S. Grant served in the Mexican War. He attained the rank of brevet captain for his outstanding service. His national notoriety came as Commander of the Union Army during the Civil War, lighting his way to the White House in 1869.

Like Grant, four other men served as active duty union officers, gaining fame and popularity, which ignited their political careers. Rutherford B. Hayes gained the rank of brevet major general. While still serving in the military he was elected to Congress. James A. Garfield joined the 42nd Ohio Volunteer Infantry, began as a colonel and quickly became one of the youngest brigadier generals in the Union Army. Two years later, he became a major general. In 1863, while still in the Union Army, he was elected to Congress. Benjamin Harrison joined the Union Army and was commissioned as a second lieutenant. He served with William Tecumseh Sherman and battled into Georgia. His participation in various important military engagements enabled him to rise to the rank of brevet brigadier general. William McKinley enlisted as a private with the Ohio Volunteers. He also participated in many important military engagements and obtained the rank of brevet major. McKinley actually served as an aide to General Rutherford B. Hayes.

Grant, Hayes, Garfield, Benjamin Harrison and McKinley were all born in Ohio. All five belonged to the Republican Party. Grant, Hayes and Garfield served as president in succession as the 18th, 19th and 20th president, respectively.

Theodore Roosevelt's political career had begun prior to serving in the military, but was greatly enhanced after organizing and leading the Rough Riders in the Spanish American War. His commanding heroics in taking San Juan Hill gained him national recognition. Shortly after his Spanish-American War duties were completed, he was elected governor of New York State.

Dwight D. Eisenhower's various high level military positions allowed him to demonstrate his gift of leadership to the world. Eisenhower served as special assistant to General MacArthur, led the WWII invasion into North Africa, became Supreme Commander of Allied Forces in Europe, advanced to army chief of staff, and in 1950 he was appointed Supreme Commander of NATO forces by President Truman. In 1952, he was elected president.

Although born into a successful and powerful family, military circumstances made John F. Kennedy a hero. During WWII, John F. Kennedy was the commanding lieutenant of PT 109. While in the Pacific, his boat was demolished by a Japanese destroyer. J.F.K. heroically saved his crew despite suffering a back injury. Pain from this injury followed him to the White House.

Military service also helped Chester Arthur on his quest of the presidency even though he had no combat duty. During the Civil War, he served as quartermaster general for New York State. His proficiency in this position gained him recognition, which led to important political appointments.

While in the navy, Jimmy Carter served under Admiral Hyman Rickover. His experiences with Admiral Rickover helped shape his future and inspired his book, *Why Not the Best?* written in 1976.

Five consecutive presidents (35th-39th), John F. Kennedy, Lyndon Johnson, Richard Nixon, Gerald Ford and Jimmy Carter all served in the U.S. Navy.

CHAPTER 4

NAMES

LAST NAMES

Some names have become quite familiar to the White House. Five pairs of presidents have shared the same last name. John Adams and John Quincy Adams were the first. This trend continued with William H. and Benjamin Harrison, Theodore and Franklin Roosevelt, Andrew and Lyndon Johnson and George H.W. and George W. Bush.

FIRST NAMES

Several chief executive first names also have been repeated. Throughout history there have been six presidents named James. James Madison began this trend, followed by James Monroe, James K. Polk, James Buchanan, James Garfield and James "Jimmy" Carter. The next most prevalent presidential first name with four is John. John Adams, John Quincy Adams, John Tyler and John F. Kennedy. There have also been four Williams. William Henry Harrison, William McKinley, William H. Taft and William Clinton. There have been three Georges. George Washington, George H.W. Bush and George W. Bush. Two presidents have been named Franklin. Franklin Roosevelt and Franklin Pierce, along with two Andrews, Andrew Jackson and Andrew Johnson.

JACKSON and JOHNSON

The two Andrews also share the fact that they were both born in the Carolinas and settled in the state of Tennessee, each have seven letters in their last name and both have the number seven in their presidential number. Andrew Jackson is president number 7 and Andrew Johnson number 17.

CLINTON

It took several tries to get a Clinton into the White House. In the election of 1792, George Washington ran unopposed, but the office of vice president became the contest. George Clinton, Revolutionary War soldier and New York governor, ran for the number two spot losing to John Adams. In 1804, George Clinton teamed up with Thomas Jefferson leading to the formation of the Democratic Party. Jefferson became president and Clinton became vice president. George Clinton's name appeared again in the 1808 election. Although he hoped to become president, he won only six electoral votes. However, he won 113 electoral votes for the vice presidency allowing him to remain as vice president. George Clinton died while in office in 1812, however this did not stop the Clinton challenges. In 1812 DeWitt Clinton, mayor of New York ran against James Madison for president. Although Madison won, Clinton came very close. Had the state of Pennsylvania voted along the same lines as the rest of the north, Clinton would have won. Finally, in 1992 a Clinton made it to the oval office with the election of Bill Clinton.

HARRISON

Even though William H. Harrison and Benjamin Harrison succeeded in making it to the presidency, another Harrison attempted to get there long before they did. Even though it was not much of a contest, in the 1792 election several men entered their names for consideration. Among them was Revolutionary War veteran Robert H. Harrison. Because of George Washington's enormous popularity, none of the other candidates even came close to winning. Harrison received only 6 electoral votes, which came from his state of Maryland.

JOHNSON

Johnson has been a popular name in the vice presidency. In 1836, Congressman Richard Johnson became Martin Van Buren's vice president. Twenty-eight years later Andrew Johnson was elected to serve as President Lincoln's vice president. Almost a century later Lyndon Johnson was chosen to fill the number two spot in the Kennedy administration. The later two Johnsons had to carry out the most dreaded duty of a vice president, the immediate transition from vice president to president upon the death of the current chief executive.

MAIDEN NAMES

Interesting name connections also extend too many of the First Ladies. John Quincy Adam's wife Louisa had the maiden name Johnson. Lyndon Johnson's wife Claudia (Lady Bird) had the maiden name of Taylor. Eleanor Roosevelt's maiden name was Roosevelt. Barbara Bush's maiden name is Pierce.

MADISON and LINCOLN

James Madison and Abraham Lincoln both married women with the last name of Todd. Dolly Madison was the widow of John Todd when she married James Madison. Todd was Mary Todd Lincoln's maiden name.

Another coincidental name involves Abraham Lincoln's stepmother. In 1819, Abraham Lincoln's widowed father married a widow by the name of Sally Johnson. Sally Johnson was born Sally Bush.

MADISON and CLINTON

Two presidents have middle names that are the same as two other presidents surnames. Ronald Wilson Reagan and William Jefferson Clinton.

NAME CHANGE

President Hiram Grant? President Leslie King? President William Blythe? No, these are not names of fictitious presidents portrayed in the movies, TV or a novel. These are the birth names of some actual U.S. presidents.

Young Hiram Ulysses Grant applied for appointment at West Point and an error led to his name being registered as Ulysses S. Grant. The mistake was never rectified and he was forever known by the second name.

Little Leslie King was born July 14, 1913 to a caring mother and a domestically violent father. Shortly after his birth, Leslie's mother fled from the abusive home taking her son with her. Three years later, she married a Michigan salesman who raised Leslie as his own son. He legally adopted Leslie and they changed his name to Gerald R. Ford Jr.

Three months before William Blythe was born, his father was killed in an automobile accident. Four years later, his mother Virginia was remarried to an Arkansas car dealer named Roger Clinton. Hence, little William Blythe's name was changed to William Clinton.

Grover Cleveland was given the birth name of Stephen Grover Cleveland, but dropped the first name in his late teens.

Calvin Coolidge was born John Calvin Coolidge, but dispensed of his first name after college.

Woodrow Wilson was originally named Thomas Woodrow Wilson after his grandfather. Like Grover and Calvin, he got rid of the first name at a young age.

Named after his father, David Dwight Eisenhower eventually began going by Dwight David Eisenhower to avoid family confusion.

Rosalynn Carter's first name is Eleanor. Rosalynn is really her middle name. This makes her the second first lady with the first name of Eleanor. Both of these first ladies have ties to Georgia. President and Mrs. Roosevelt had the Little White House in Warm Springs, Georgia. President and Mrs. Carter are native to Plains, Georgia.

CHAPTER 5

FUTURE PRESIDENTS SERVING SITTING PRESIDENTS

Throughout American history, many men who went on to become president served under an existing president in some official capacity. At the time of their service to the president, it is likely that some of these men felt the dream and desire to one day become the leader of the world's greatest nation. Others never dreamt that destiny would take them there.

John Adams, the second president, was the first future president to serve a sitting president. He served as George Washington's vice president for the entire duration of the Washington administration.

Thomas Jefferson served George Washington as secretary of state. He then became vice president to John Adams giving him adequate experience to become the third president. Upon becoming president, Jefferson appointed James Madison as his secretary of state.

In 1809 Madison became the fourth president, and made the future fifth president, James Monroe, his secretary of state and secretary of war. Monroe also served as an ambassador under Thomas Jefferson securing the Louisiana Purchase from France.

John Quincy Adams accompanied his father on several important political missions. He also served as minister to the Netherlands and to Prussia under George Washington. President John Adams promoted him to the Berlin Legation. In 1808, President Madison appointed him minister to Russia. He also served yet another president by becoming President Monroe's secretary of state.

Martin Van Buren served as President Andrew Jackson's secretary of state and later was elected to the vice presidency for Jackson's second term.

President Adams appointed William Henry Harrison governor of the New Indiana territory in 1800, forty-one years prior to his brief service as the ninth president.

John Tyler served as William Henry Harrison's vice president for one month before making a place in history by becoming the first vice president to become president through the death of his predecessor.

In 1845, General Zachary Taylor carried out orders from President James K. Polk to make military presence known in the disputed Texas-Mexico territory. This maneuver ignited the Mexican War and made General Taylor a national hero, which led him to the presidency.

Millard Fillmore was elected as Zachary Taylor's vice president and served the former military hero for a short sixteen months before becoming president himself.

Prior to becoming the fifteenth president, James Buchanan was appointed secretary of state by James K. Polk. However, more politically significant for Buchanan was serving his predecessor, President Franklin Pierce as minister of Britain. While filling this position he was a participant in drafting the Ostend Manifesto, which made him popular with the South, and helped in his own presidential election.

Andrew Johnson served Abraham Lincoln in two capacities. In 1862, Lincoln appointed Johnson military governor of Tennessee. He served faithfully in that position before joining Lincoln as his vice president.

Ulysses S. Grant served President Lincoln as commander of the Union armies.

Chester Arthur was appointed collector of customs for the port of New York in 1871 by President Grant. He also served President James Garfield as vice president for nine short months before becoming president himself.

After Chester Arthur, no future president worked directly for a president until an energetic Theodore Roosevelt made himself known. In 1897, President McKinley appointed Roosevelt assistant secretary of the navy. Three years later Roosevelt was placed on the ticket to be McKinley's vice president. He served as McKinley's vice president for six months before becoming president himself.

William H. Taft was appointed civil governor of the Philippines in 1900 by President McKinley. In 1904, Taft accepted the position of secretary of war in Theodore Roosevelt's cabinet. Defeated by Woodrow Wilson in the election of 1912, Taft left the presidency, however he continued to be of service to his country. In 1921, President Harding appointed Taft chief justice of the Supreme Court giving Taft the job he had always wanted.

Calvin Coolidge was chosen as Warren Harding's 1920 running mate, making him vice president for slightly less than two and a half years before becoming president himself.

Herbert Hoover was appointed United States food administrator during World War I by President Woodrow Wilson. Hoover's ability to carry out this position with skill and accuracy helped to win the war. He was later appointed secretary of commerce under President Harding. Fourteen years after leaving the presidency, Hoover again received appointments from other presidents. After World War II President Harry Truman appointed him honorary chairman of the Famine Emergency Committee to aid starving people of Europe and Asia. In 1948, former President Hoover was again selected by President Truman to chair the bipartisan commission on Organization of the Executive Branch of the Government, known as the Hoover Commission. Again, in 1953 then President Dwight Eisenhower appointed Hoover to head a second Hoover Commission.

A young Franklin D. Roosevelt was assistant secretary of the navy under President Woodrow Wilson several years before becoming president. Running for his fourth term, Roosevelt chose a relatively unknown Harry S Truman as his running mate. A short time later, this unknown man became president when F.D.R. died suddenly in Warm Springs, Georgia. In 1950, President Truman appointed Dwight Eisenhower supreme commander of NATO forces.

Lyndon Johnson was appointed director of the National Youth Administration in 1935 by President Franklin Roosevelt. In 1960 he announced his own candidacy for president, but quickly realized that Senator John Kennedy was likely unbeatable for the Democratic nomination. Knowing this, Johnson accepted the nomination for vice president, serving President Kennedy until November 1963.

In 1952, young Richard Nixon accepted the nomination for vice president and worked as such for President Eisenhower for two terms. In 1973, now President Richard Nixon appointed Gerald R. Ford vice president in response to Spiro Agnew's resignation.

George H. W. Bush, prior to becoming the 41st president, served Presidents Nixon and Ford as ambassador to the United Nations, envoy to China and director of the CIA. Finally in 1980, he accepted the offer to run as Ronald Reagan's vice president and retained that position for two terms.

George W. Bush, prior to becoming the 43rd president, unofficially aided his father by working extensively on his presidential campaign in 1988 and again in his 1992 bid for re-election.

CHAPTER 6

PRESIDENTIAL INSPIRATION

Many events great and small have planted the seed in a young boy or a young man that caused him to desire the presidency. One can only wonder what influential event spurred the stamina necessary to endure the sacrifices it takes to run for president and subsequently run a nation. The following events, coincidences and circumstances changed and made history.

CALL ME MR. PRESIDENT...AGAIN

Prior to becoming president of the United States, some men were already used to the title of President. These men had already achieved the pinnacle title in the private sector as president of companies, organizations and institutions.

In 1908 Woodrow Wilson was president of Princeton University. While holding this post he was elected governor of New Jersey, which helped put him on the road to the White House.

After serving as Army Chief of Staff, Dwight Eisenhower accepted the presidency of Columbia University in 1948. At the same time, Ronald Reagan was serving as president of the Screen Actors Guild.

George H. W. Bush, prior to entering politics, was President of Zupata Petroleum Company in Houston, Texas.

INFLUENTIAL MEETINGS

At the age of five years old, Franklin Roosevelt met then President Grover Cleveland. Ironically, it is reported that upon meeting young Franklin, President Cleveland told him "...I wish for you that you may never be president..."

In July 1963, sixteen-year-old Bill Clinton was one of several Boy's Nation participants chosen for academic achievement to travel to Washington D.C. These young men were dubbed future leaders of the free world. On July 24, Bill Clinton and his group attended a speech given by President John Kennedy in the Rose Garden at the White House. Sitting in the front row, young Bill was the first to shake the president's hand immediately after the speech. Bill Clinton's mother often said that this meeting started Bill's political interest and ambitions.

At age twenty-nine, Lyndon Johnson met President Franklin Roosevelt. President Roosevelt came to Galveston, Texas to campaign for young L.B.J. who was running for Congress. Johnson ran for the House of Representatives on the New Deal platform and won the election.

In 1971, then Governor Jimmy Carter and Rosalynn Carter met President Richard Nixon. According to his book *White House Diary*, Carter states that this meeting had a "lasting impact" and in part caused him to keep a diary during his presidency.

CHAPTER 7

RELATIVES AND RELATIONSHIPS

RELATIVES

Along with the well-known Adams and Bush father-son relationships, there are many other genetic White House connections.

Benjamin Harrison was grandson to William Henry Harrison.

Eleanor Roosevelt was Teddy Roosevelt's niece. She was also sixth cousin to her husband Franklin.

Barbara Bush is a descendent of Franklin Pierce. Her maiden name was Pierce.

Zachary Taylor's daughter married Jefferson Davis. Several years after Taylor's death, his son-in-law became president of the Confederacy during the Civil War.

John Adams was third cousin to his wife Abigail.

John Quincy Adams was third cousin once removed to his mother Abigail.

President Nixon's daughter Julie married Dwight Eisenhower's grandson David Eisenhower. President Eisenhower secured his grandson's name in presidential history by naming the presidential retreat Camp David after him.

Martin Van Buren's son Abraham married Dolly Madison's cousin Angelica Singleton. Angelica became the official hostess of the White House for her widowed father-in-law, fulfilling the same duties as her famous first lady cousin.

George Washington was a half first cousin twice removed of James Madison.

Theodore Roosevelt was third cousin twice removed to Martin Van Buren and fifth cousin of Franklin Roosevelt.

John Tyler was a great-(3)uncle of Harry Truman.

Zachary Taylor was second cousin to James Madison and fourth cousin three times removed of Franklin Roosevelt.

Ulysses Grant was a sixth cousin once removed of Grover Cleveland and fourth cousin once removed of Franklin Roosevelt.

Richard Nixon was a seventh cousin twice removed of William Taft and an eighth cousin once removed of Herbert Hoover.

George H .W. Bush and George W. Bush are both distant cousins of Franklin Pierce, Theodore Roosevelt, Abraham Lincoln and Gerald Ford.

RELATIONSHIPS

Alphonso Taft, father of William H. Taft served as secretary of war and later, attorney general in President Grant's Cabinet.

William H. Taft's father-in-law, Judge John W. Herron, was a law partner of Rutherford B. Hayes.

Robert Todd Lincoln, son of Abraham Lincoln served as James Garfield's and Chester Arthur's secretary of war. He also served as minister to Great Britian for Benjamin Harrison.

Frederick Dent Grant, son of Ulysses S. Grant served as minister to Austria-Hungary for Benjamin Harrison. He replaced Theodore Roosevelt as New York City police commissioner in 1897, and later served as assistant war secretary for William McKinley.

Martin Van Buren dated Ellen Randolph, Thomas Jefferson's granddaughter. She eventually married a man with the last name of Coolidge.

When Andrew Johnson wed his wife Eliza, the officiating clergyman was Mordecai Lincoln, a relative of Abraham Lincoln.

In 1905 Harry Truman roomed at a boarding house in Kansas City with Dwight Eisenhower's brother Arthur.

CHAPTER 8

WASHINGTON TO OBAMA

1. George Washington

    Washington was the only president unanimously elected by the Electoral College.

    He was the only president that never lived in the White House. Ironically, when he met his future wife Martha Custis, the name of her estate was the White House.

2. John Adams

    Adams was the first president to reside in the White House.

    He was the first vice president.

3. Thomas Jefferson

    In 1807, Jefferson signed into law a bill that prohibited the importation of slaves, even though he was a slave owner.

    Prior to his death, Jefferson wrote his own epitaph for his tombstone which mentioned he was the author of the Declaration of Independence, of the Statue of Virginia for Religious Freedom and the Father of the University of Virginia. He did not mention that he was president.

4. James Madison

    At five feet four inches tall, he was the shortest president. At only one hundred pounds, he was the lightest president.

    Madison had no children.

5. James Monroe

    In 1820 President Monroe ran unopposed for re-election. However, one electoral vote was cast for John Quincy Adams.

    Thomas Jefferson designed Monroe's home in Virginia.

6. John Quincy Adams

    Adams was the first former president to be elected to public office. He was elected to Congress in 1831.

    He died at the U.S. Capital.

    Adams first son was named George Washington Adams.

7. Andrew Jackson

    Jackson was the first president to experience an assassination attempt.

    While attending services for a deceased congressman at the U.S. Capital, an assailant attempted to shoot the president, but the gun misfired. Jackson rushed the would be assassin in order to strike him with his cane. The man fired again with a second gun, which also misfired. Many people rushed to Jackson's aid. One of the people that helped secure the gunman was Davey Crocket, a congressman himself at the time.

8. Martin Van Buren

    Born December 5, 1782, he was the first president born an American citizen.

    While Van Buren was Andrew Jackson's vice president, Jackson was so intent on seeing Van Buren succeed him, he considered resigning.

9. William Henry Harrison

    Harrison was the only president to go to medical school, however, he chose a military career instead.

    His father was defeated for the Virginia State legislature by John Tyler's father.

10. John Tyler

    Tyler fathered the most children of any president. He had fourteen offspring that lived to maturity.

    After becoming president, as a result of William Henry Harrison's death, Tyler refused to open any mail addressed to "acting president".

    In 1861 former President Tyler was elected to the Confederate House of Representatives, but he died before he could serve.

11. James K. Polk

    Polk's great-great granduncle John Knox was the founder of Presbyterianism.

    He was the only former speaker of the House to become president.

12. Zachary Taylor

    Taylor was supposed to be sworn in as president on March 4, 1849, however, this was a Sunday and he refused to take oath of office until the following day. President Polk's term expired on March 4, 1849. Therefore, some say that technically David Atchison who was president of the senate was president for a day.

13. Millard Fillmore

    Fillmore met his future wife Abigail, because she was his teacher.

    He refused an honorary law degree from Oxford stating, "I have not the advantage of a classical education, and no man should in my judgment accept a degree he cannot read".

14. Franklin Pierce

    President Pierce's secretary of war was Jefferson Davis. Ironically, Davis was good at his job and improved the army a great deal. This improved army would defeat Davis's cause in the Civil War ten years later.

15. James Buchanan

    Buchanan was the only president that never married.

    He is the only president from Pennsylvania.

16. Abraham Lincoln

    Just prior to being assassinated, one of the last official acts President Lincoln did was to sign legislation for the formation of The Secret Service.

    At six feet four inches, Lincoln was the tallest president.

17. Andrew Johnson

    As vice president, Johnson was a Democrat serving under a Republican president.

Johnson's father worked as a janitor at a bank run by William Polk, a cousin of James K. Polk.

Johnson never attended a single day of formal schooling. With the help of his wife, he taught himself to read and write.

18. Ulysses S. Grant

As a young soldier in the Mexican War, a superior officer reprimanded Grant for looking shoddy. Grant was humiliated by this incident and never forgot it, which was unfortunate for the reprimanding officer. The officer was Robert E. Lee.

Grant was the first president whose parents both lived to see him enter office.

19. Rutherford B. Hayes

As a congressman, Hayes voted for Andrew Johnson's impeachment.

In 1875, Hayes defeated Alphonso Taft, President Taft's father for the Ohio gubernatorial nomination.

20. James Garfield

Garfield could write in Latin with one hand and Greek with the other hand at the same time.

Like his presidential predessesor Rutherford Hayes, Garfield was elected to Congress while still serving in the military.

21. Chester Arthur

Arthur was always known to be impeccably dressed no matter what the occasion.

Appointed collector for the port of New York by President Grant in 1871, Arthur was removed from that post by President Hayes in 1878.

22. Grover Cleveland

As a young man, Cleveland was sheriff of Erie County, New York. As sheriff, he personally executed two convicted men.

Cleveland served as mayor of Buffalo, New York, governor of New York and president of the United States all within three and a half years.

23. Benjamin Harrison

John Harrison, Benjamin Harrison's father is the only man to be the son of one president and the father of another.

First Lady Caroline Harrison died just two weeks before President Harrison was defeated for re-election. In 1896, former president Harrison married Mary Scott Lord Dimmick, Caroline's niece.

24. Grover Cleveland

In 1882 prior to becoming president, Grover Cleveland was mayor of Buffalo, New York. Nineteen years later Cleveland's successor William McKinley was assassinated there.

25. William McKinley

McKinley was the last Civil War veteran to become president.

His first term vice president Garret Hobart died while in office, causing McKinley to choose Teddy Roosevelt for his 1900 campaign running mate.

26. Theodore Roosevelt

At age 42, Roosevelt was the youngest man to become president.

His maternal great great grandfather Archibald Bullock was a delegate from Georgia to the Continental Congress and served as president of Georgia during the Revolution.

Roosevelt was blind in his left eye, because of a boxing injury.

27. William H. Taft

Taft is the only former president to administer the oath of office to an incoming president. As chief justice, he administered the oath to Calvin Coolidge and Herbert Hoover.

At three hundred thirty two pounds, Taft was the heaviest president.

28. Woodrow Wilson

Due to poor health as a child, learning was difficult for Wilson and he was unable to read until about age nine. Nevertheless, he is the only president to earn a Ph.D.

29. Warren Harding

The 1920 election, which Harding won, was the first that allowed women to vote.

Harding was the first to be taken to his inauguration by automobile.

30. Calvin Coolidge

Coolidge was born on July 4, 1872.

Upon the death of President Harding, Vice President Coolidge was given the oath of office by his father who was a notary.

31. Herbert Hoover

Hoover never took a salary as president.

Hoover donated money to Theodore Roosevelt's 1912 third party campaign.

32. Franklin Roosevelt

F.D.R. was the longest serving president.

In 1921, Roosevelt was stricken with polio. He was first seen medically by Dr. W. Keen. In 1893, Dr. Keen took part in a top-secret cancer operation on President Grover Cleveland.

Roosevelt appointed the first woman cabinet member. He appointed Frances Perkins as secretary of labor.

33. Harry Truman

Truman's middle initial S was his entire middle name.

President Truman chose not to run for a third term, restoring the traditional two terms that was interrupted by F.D.R.

34. Dwight D. Eisenhower

   Eisenhower had five brothers. All six were at one time or another nicknamed Ike.

   Eisenhower was a skilled artist, chef and poker player.

35. John F. Kennedy

   J.F.K. was the first president born in the twentieth century.

   At age 43 Kennedy was the youngest person elected to the presidency.

   Lincoln was the last name of President Kennedy's personal secretary.

36. Lyndon Johnson

   Lyndon Johnson was born in 1908. Andrew Johnson was born in 1808.

   At six feet three inches tall, Lyndon Johnson was the second tallest president.

37. Richard M. Nixon

   Nixon was the only president to resign.

   Nixon's father, Frank Nixon met President McKinley.
   Prior to that, he had been a strict Democrat.
   He was so impressed with McKinley he started voting Republican.

38. Gerald R. Ford

   Ford is the only person to have held the office of vice president and of president without being elected to either.

   There were two separate assasination attempts on President Ford in September 1975. Both assailants were women. The president was not harmed in either incident.

39. Jimmy Carter

   Carter is the first president born in a hospital.

   He is the only president to teach Sunday school before, during and after his presidency.

Carter is the only president to auction off one of his own original paintings. He filled in as auctioneer when his painting came up for bid at a charity auction in Plains, Pennsylvania.

President Carter has lived the most number of years after leaving the White House than any other president.

He has written more books than any other president and is the only one to have written a novel.

40. Ronald Reagan

Reagan was the first president to appoint a woman to the Supreme Court.

Reagan was the oldest president in office. He was 77 years old when he left the White House.

41. George H.W. Bush

President Bush and his wife Barbara both have Grave's disease, a thyroid disorder.

Bush is a tenth cousin once removed of his vice president, Dan Quayle.

42. Bill Clinton

Clinton has become very close friends with his former rival George H.W. Bush.

As a young man in Arkansas, Clinton was elected governor, lost the bid for re-election and then won the seat back in the following election.

43. George W. Bush

Bush is a descendent of president number fourteen, Franklin Pierce, and the transposed number forty-one, George H.W. Bush.

Bush's 2000 presidential victory over Al Gore was so close it was finally settled by the U.S. Supreme Court.

44. Barack Obama

Obama is the first African-American to be elected president.

President Obama is the first president to have a former first lady in his cabinet. Hillary Clinton was secretary of state in the president's first term.

CHAPTER 9

COLLECTIBLES

Select items from the authors collection.

Celluloid photo album with photo of
Teddy Roosevelt in Rough Rider Uniform. Circa 1898.

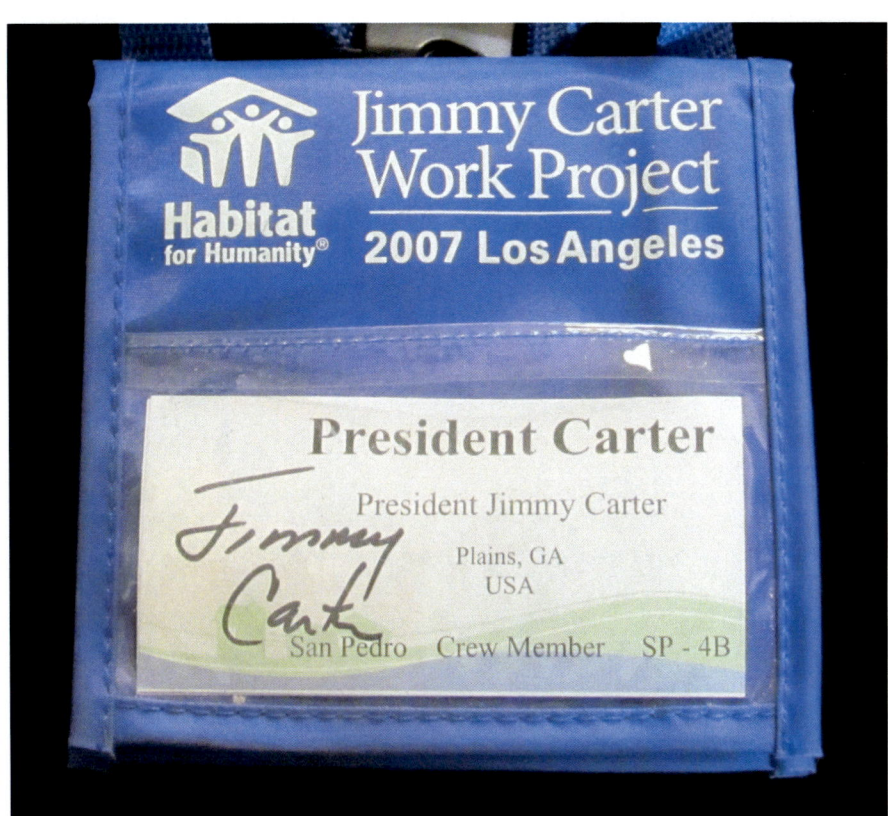

Jimmy Carter's
Habitat for Humanity
crew member ID.
Hand signed.
Circa 2007.

Rosalynn Carter's
Arctic Expedition
for Climate Action
I.D. badge.
Hand signed.

Pottery and cork bottle stoppers.
Harry S Truman, General McArthur and Winston Churchill. Circa 1940's.

Ronald Reagan name card as Governor. Hand signed. Circa 1980.

Paper Martin Van Buren campaign card from the 1840 campaign in which he was defeated by William Henry Harrison.

Pulling the tab which says
A Beautiful Goblet of White-House Champagne changes Van Buren to a frown and says
An Ugly Mug of Log Cabin Hard Cider.

Cigar presented to President Jimmy Carter by Cuban leader Fidel Castro. Shadow box framed.

Whiskey bottles.

William McKinley photo. Hand signed. Circa 1900.

White House press bag. Circa 1960's.

Murano glass paperweight.
J.F.K.
Circa 1964.

38

Metal clock depicting F.D.R. at the wheel. Circa 1940.

Benjamin Harrison
trade card.
Circa 1890.

Harrison and Morton
lapel ribbon.
1888 campaign.

40

John F. Kennedy stationary from campaign headquarters. 1960 campaign.

Hat owned and worn by
Jimmy Carter.
Habitat for Humanity.
Jimmy and Rosalynn
Carter work project.
Hand signed by
Rosalynn Carter &
Jimmy Carter.
Circa 2009.

Air Evac Lifeteam hat.
Owned by Jimmy Carter.
Hand signed on brim.

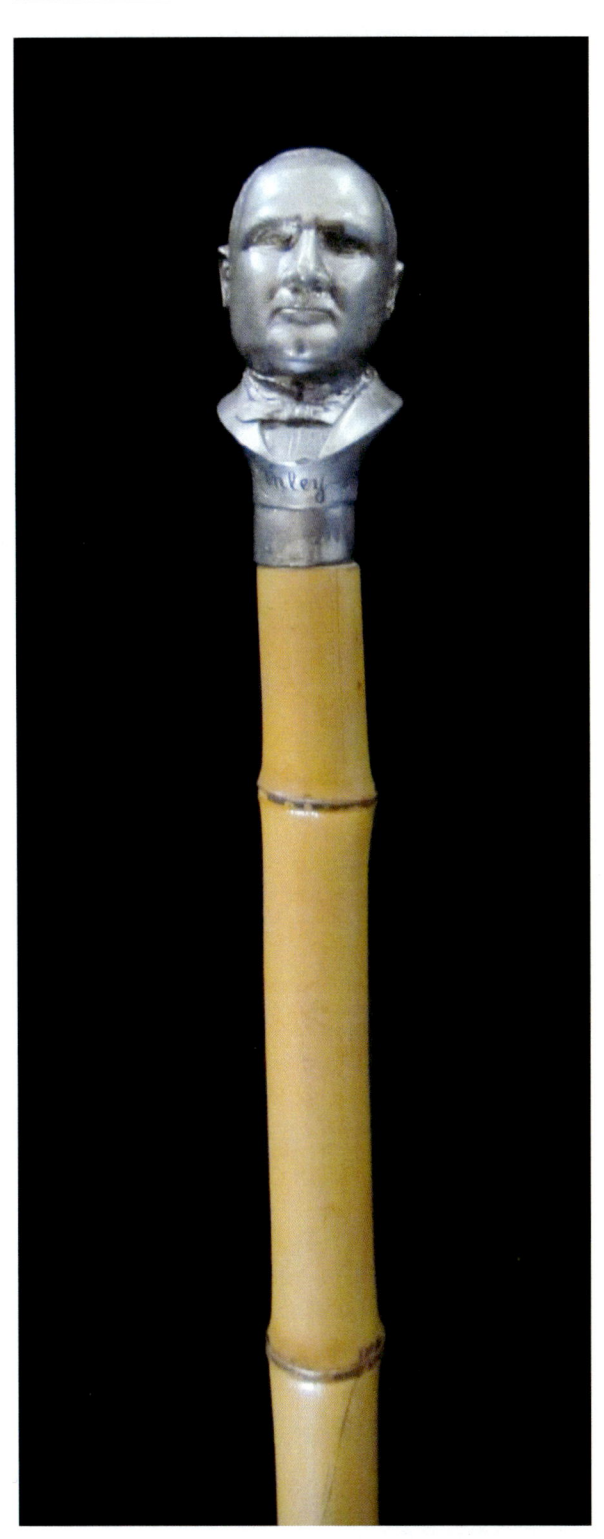

William McKinley campaign cane.
Circa 1896.

White House champagne bottle never opened.
Circa 1980's or 1990's.

Grover Cleveland campaign poster
for New York State Governor.
Circa 1882.

Prototype stained glass window. Measures 14 inches by 10 inches.
This miniature window was made as a design prototype for a 6 foot by 3 foot window
for the Historic Inn in Plains, Georgia. The prototype and the project windows
were designed and made by Kasmark & Marshall in Luzerne, Pa. 2011

Wooden flip coin.
1980 campaign.

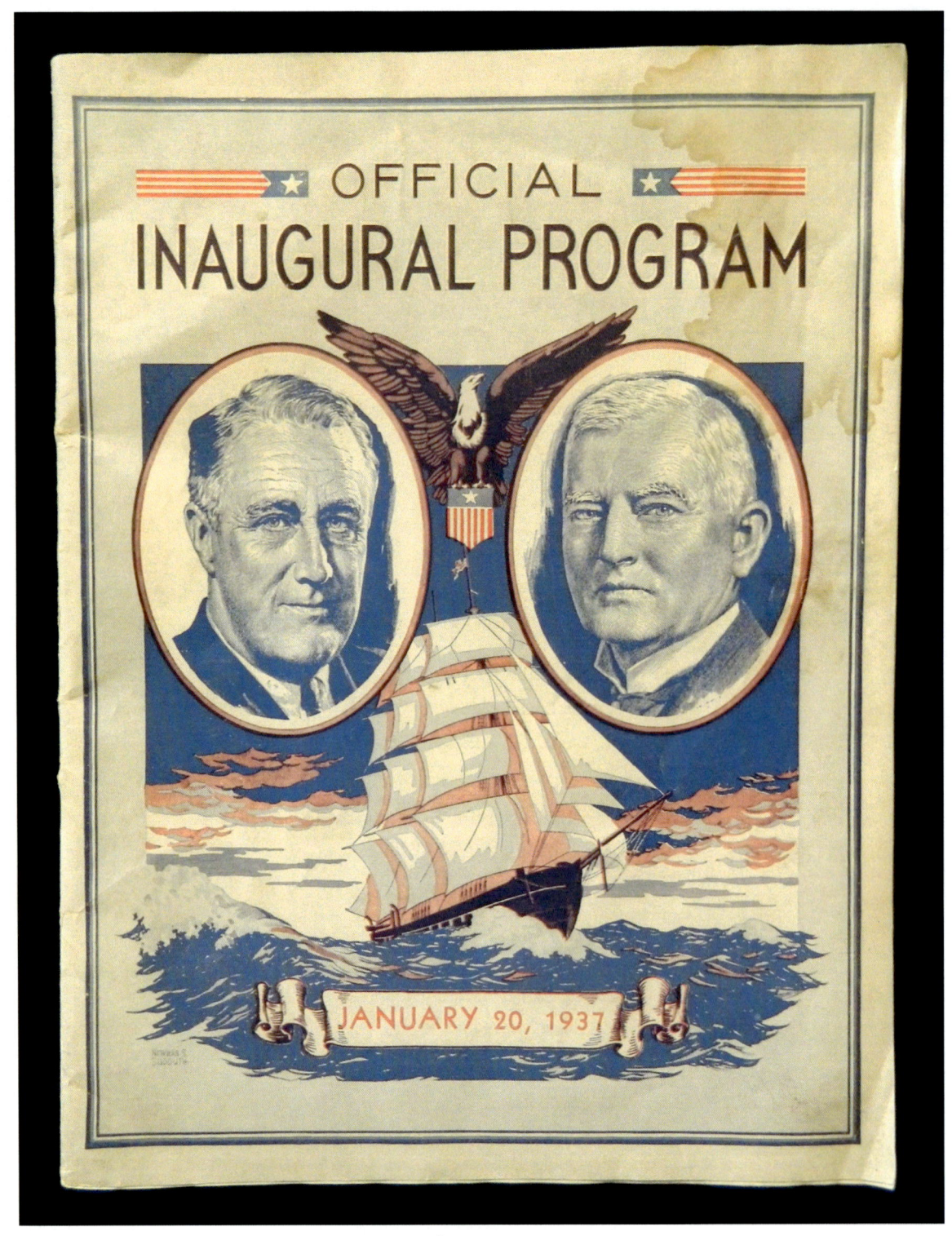

Inaugural Program. 1937.

Book personally owned by Franklin Roosevelt. Bird City by E.A. McIlhenny. Given to Roosevelt by McIlhenny 1934.

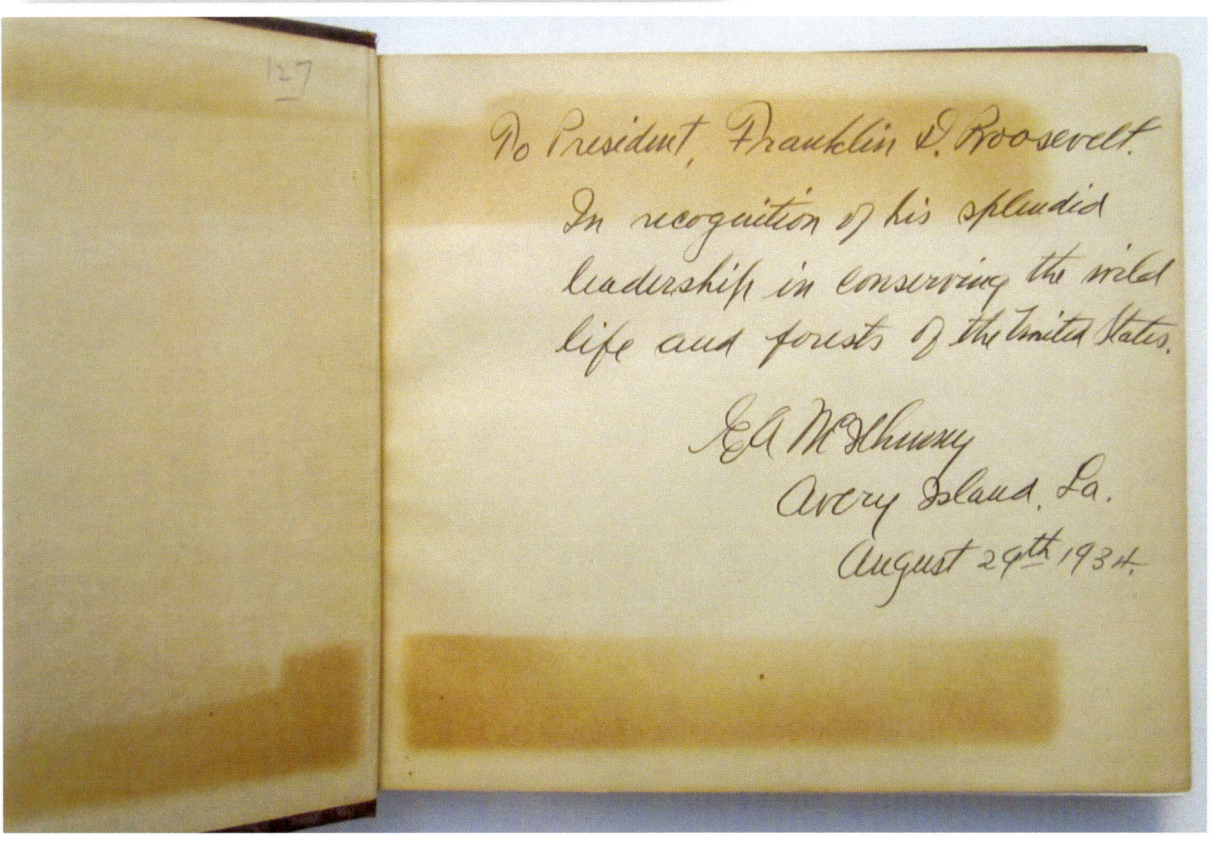

To President, Franklin D. Roosevelt.

In recognition of his splendid leadership in conserving the wild life and forests of the United States.

E A McIlhenny
Avery Island, La.
August 29th 1934.

White House program and small Mexican flag for Mexican President Fox's
September 5, 2001 visit with George W. Bush.

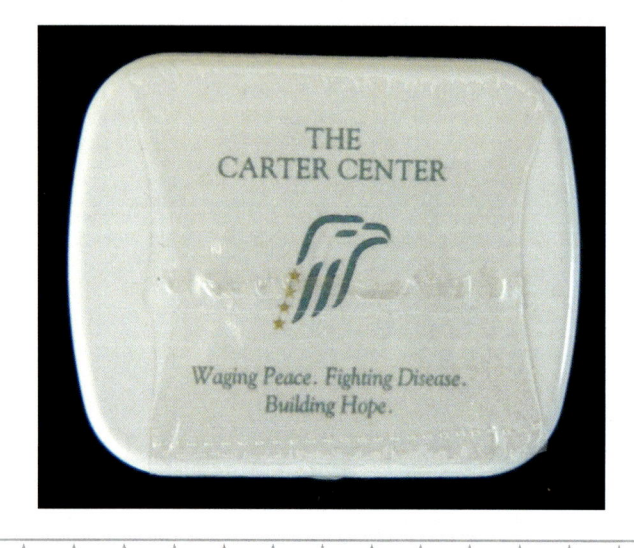

Box of mints.
The Carter Center.

Campaign button proof design on paper.

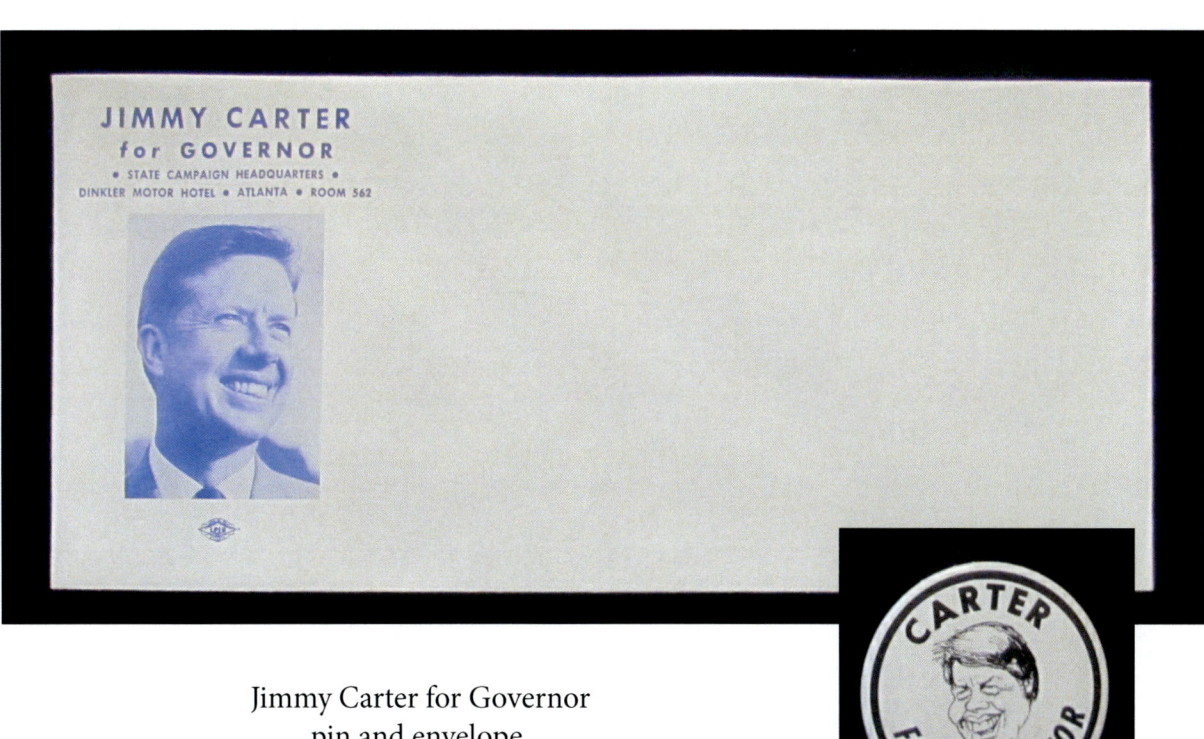

Jimmy Carter for Governor
pin and envelope.
Circa 1970.

49

Eisenhower lighter from
1956 campaign picnic.

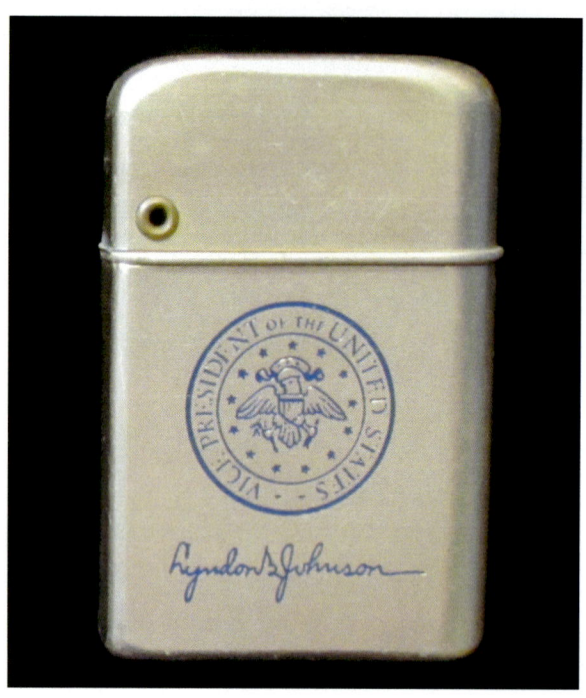

Lyndon Johnson vice president lighter.
Circa 1961.

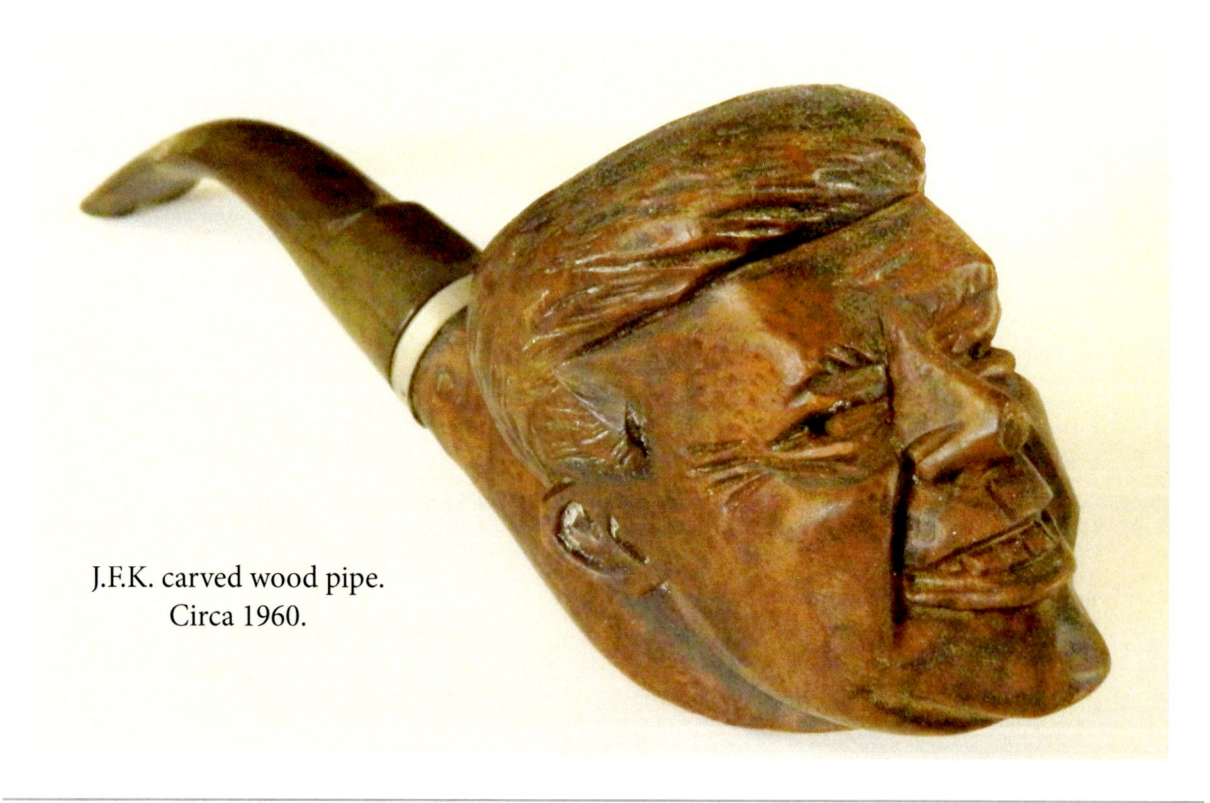

J.F.K. carved wood pipe.
Circa 1960.

William Henry Harrison campaign scarf. Circa 1840.

Pencil with Herbert Hoover eraser. Circa 1928.

51

Republican and Democrat paper ballots. 1864 election.

Lincoln mourning ribbon, cloth.
Circa 1865.

Coca-Cola bottle.
Special edition for the grand opening of
the Plains, Georgia Historic Inn.
The Inn is managed by Jan Williams,
Amy Carter's former school teacher.

Early transferware plate
showing the White House.
On reverse
The Presidents House Washington.
Circa 1830.

Tin Litho tray. Circa 1901.

White House Souvenirs. Plate seven and a half inches. Circa 1890.

Mug. Circa 1900.

Selection of Eisenhower campaign buttons.

Miniature folk art wood carving
of Abraham Lincoln.
Two inches top to bottom. Circa 1865.

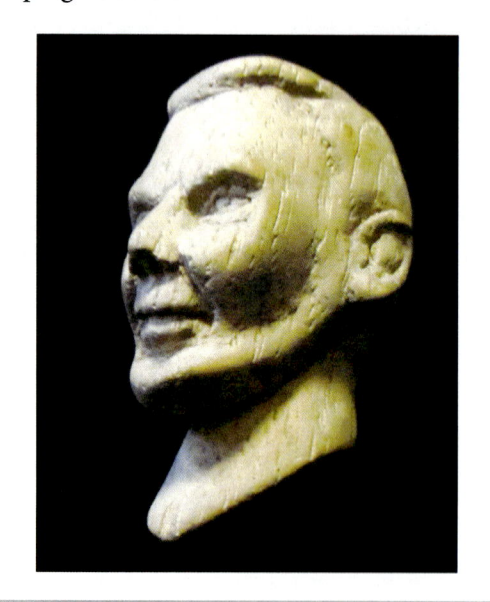

1969 Inauguration No Parking Sign.

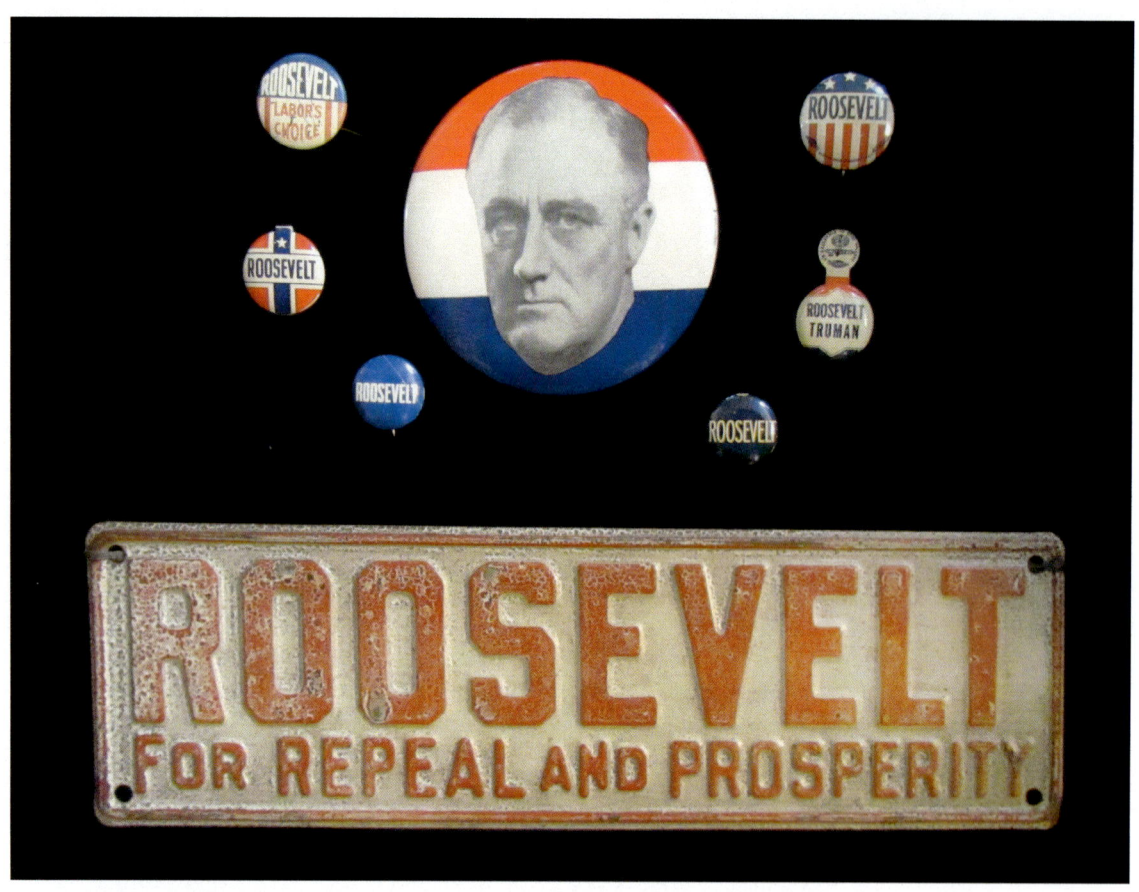

Selection of F.D.R. campaign buttons. Tin sign Roosevelt for Repeal and Prosperity.

Campaign card. Nixon-Lodge and Pennsylvania Candidates. 1960.

Introduction to Medicare Part D booklet.
Hand signed by Bill Clinton and Hillary Rodham Clinton.

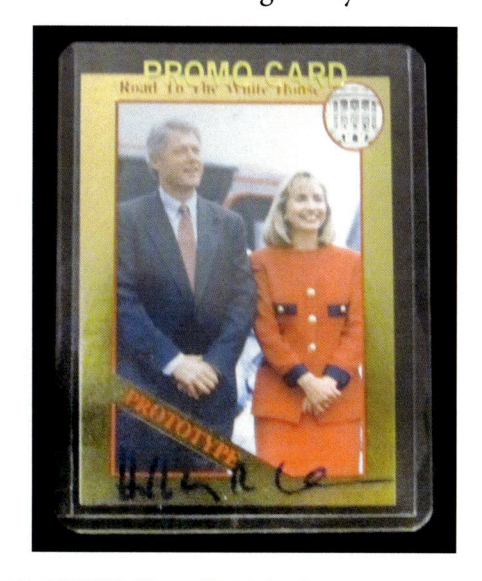

Prototype trading card.
Hand signed by
Hillary Clinton.

Iron pull toy depicting Teddy Roosevelt leading the Rough Riders. Circa 1898.

U.S. Secret Service Medals. 2012 Republican and Democratic conventions.

Pamplet showing
Herbert Hoover on the front.
Contains facts and figures.
Circa 1928.

Sewing kit
showing Herbert Hoover
on the front.
Campaign item for
the 1928 election.

Placemat showing the Nixon family. Circa 1968.

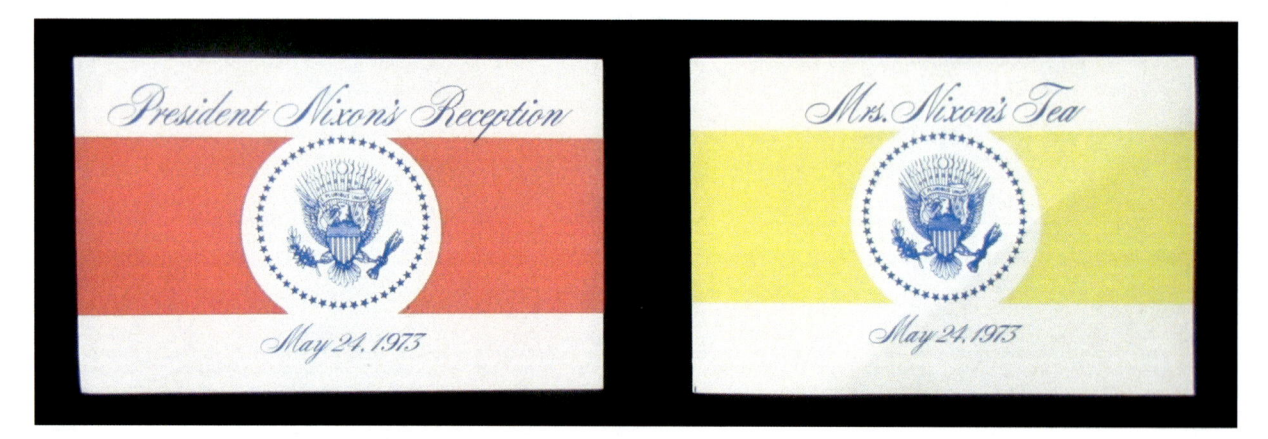

Place cards for White House Reception May 1973.

Campaign sheet music for Woodrow Wilson.
Circa 1916.

Sheet music. Abraham Lincoln.
Dated 1926.

Book card.
Decision Points.
Hand signed by
George W. Bush.
2010.

Die cast model of Air Force One. Hand signed by Jimmy Carter.

Booklet. Souvenir Inaugural Ball March 1889.
Contains etchings of Benjamin Harrison and Levi Morton.

Theodore Roosevelt original Bureau of War Records U.S. Army record.
Reverse side lists all of the Cuban battles he was involved in. Circa 1898.

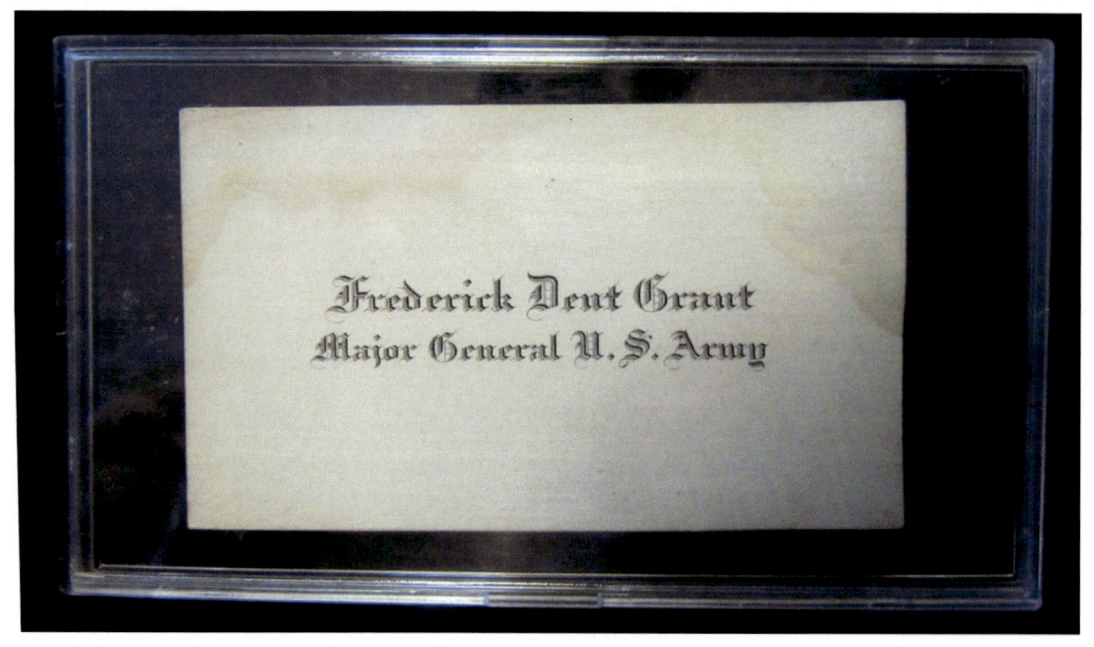

Original Spanish American War era calling card of Frederick Dent Grant, son of Ulysses S. Grant.
Circa 1898.

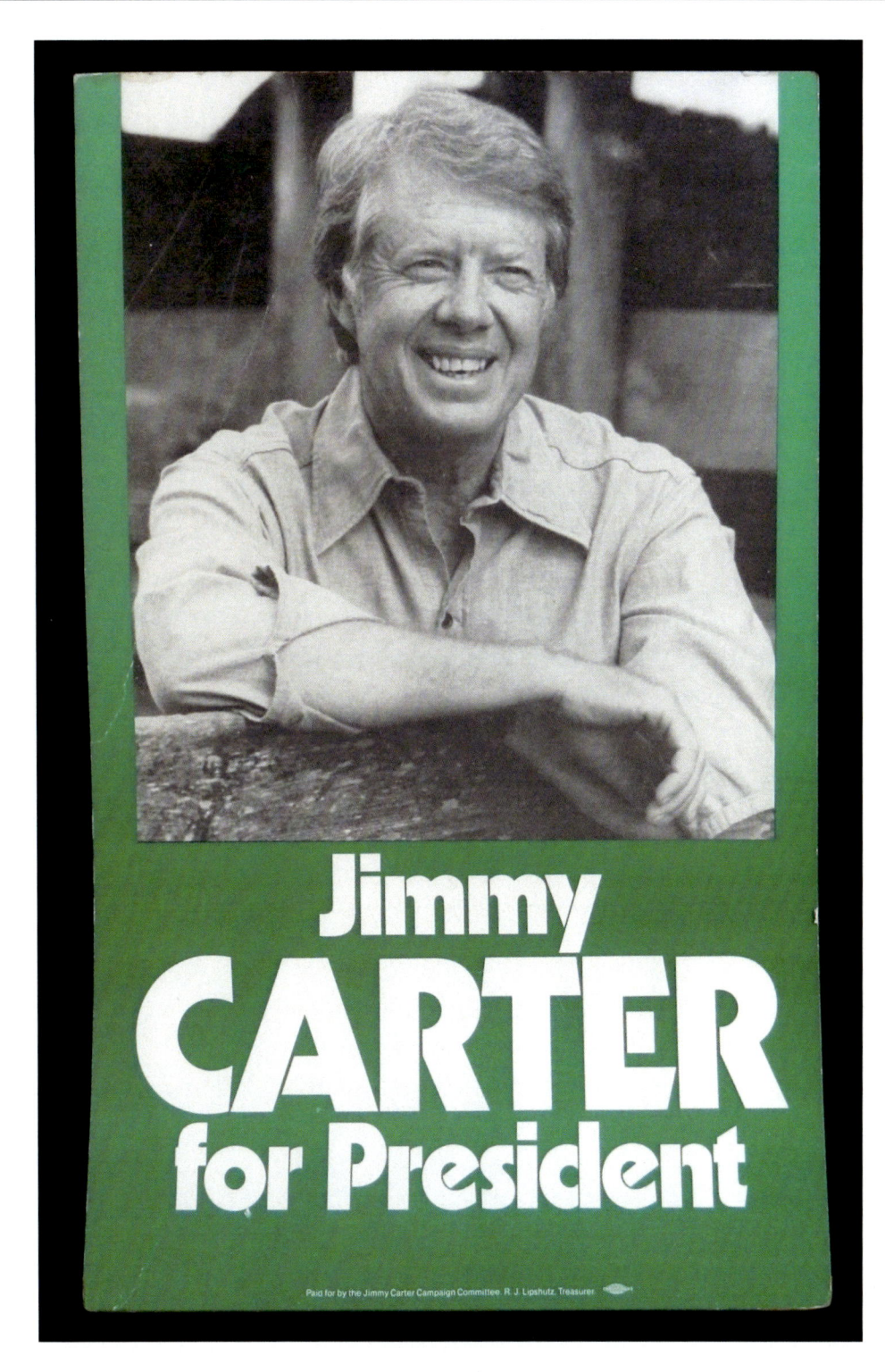

Campaign poster. 1976.

1936 Democratic National Convention ticket unused.

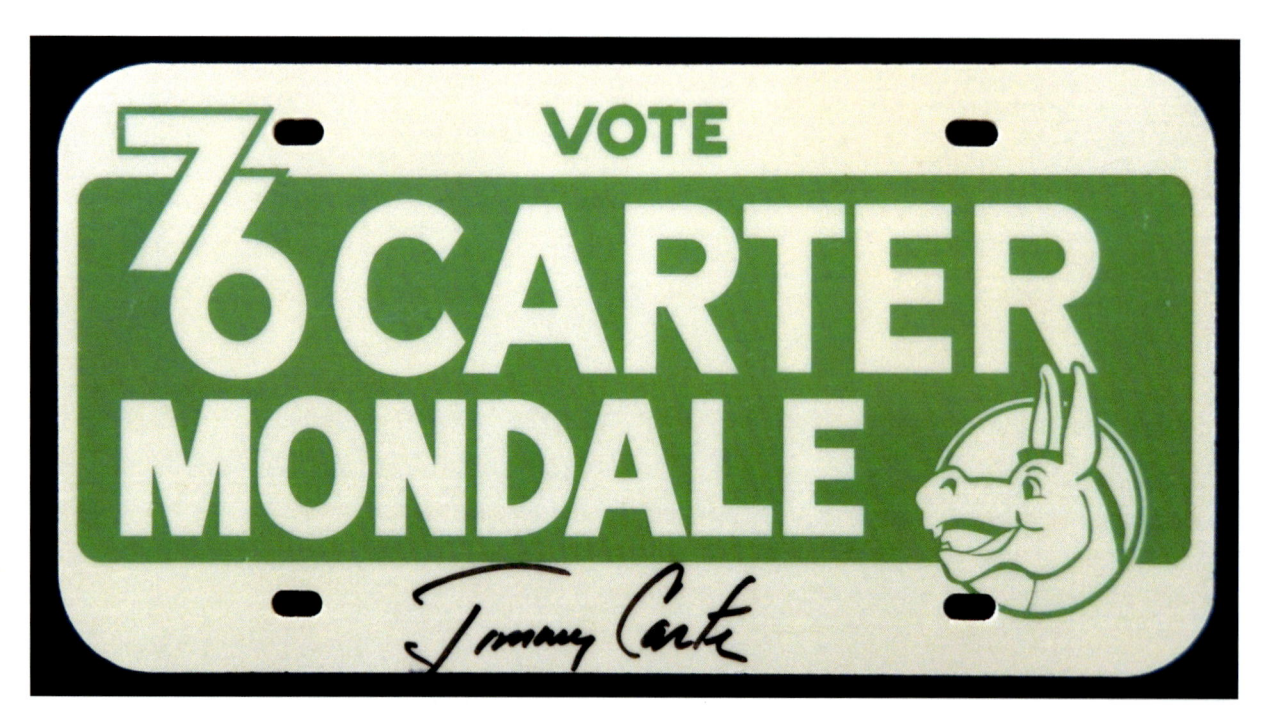

License plate campaign plaque. Hand signed by Jimmy Carter.

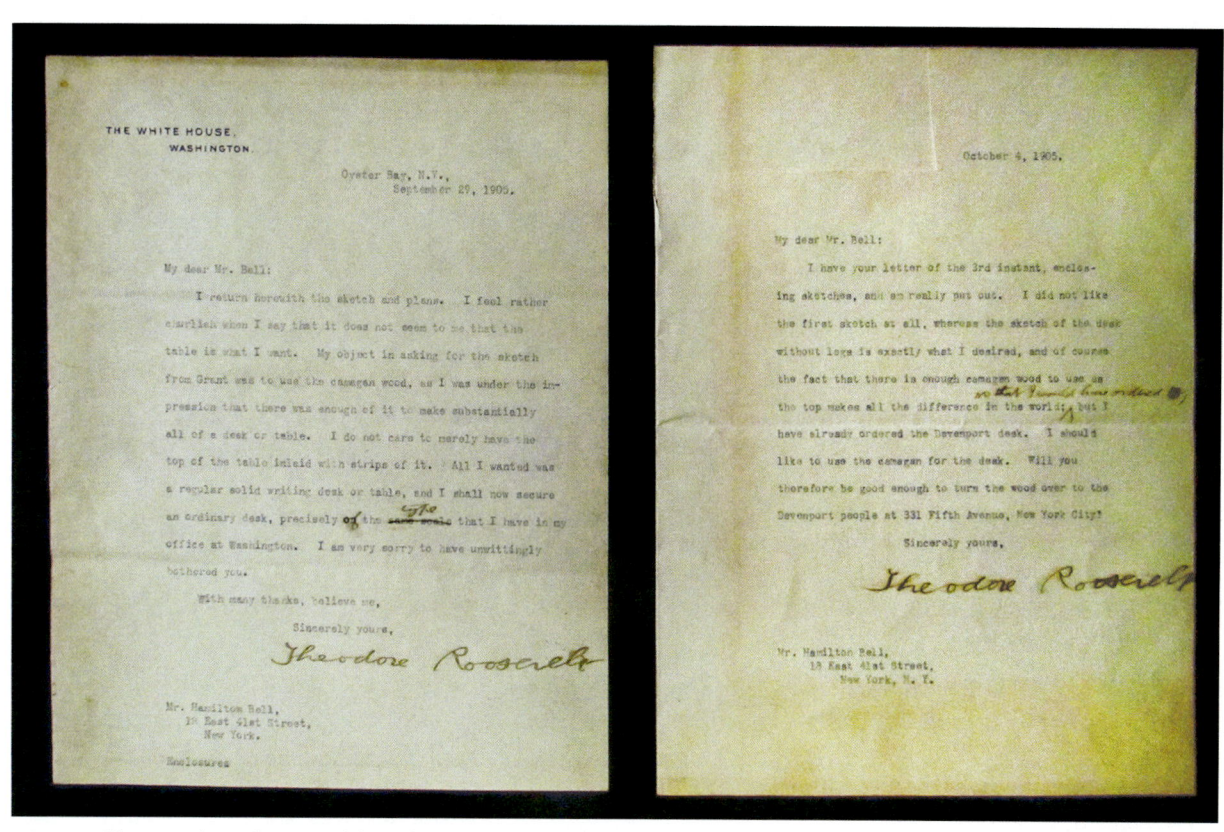

Pair of letters hand signed by Theodore Roosevelt. Letters written as president on White House stationary. Subject matter concerns having a new desk made for the president.
September and October 1905.

Cast iron boot jack
in the form of
the democratic donkey.
Underside is Impressed
"Roosevelt in 32".

69

Executive Mansion stationary.
Circa 1901.
Note the black border
as a sign of mourning for the death of William McKinley.

City of New York Police certificate.
Signed by Theodore Roosevelt as Police Commissioner July 1895.

Mustache cup.
Porcelain.
Circa 1904.

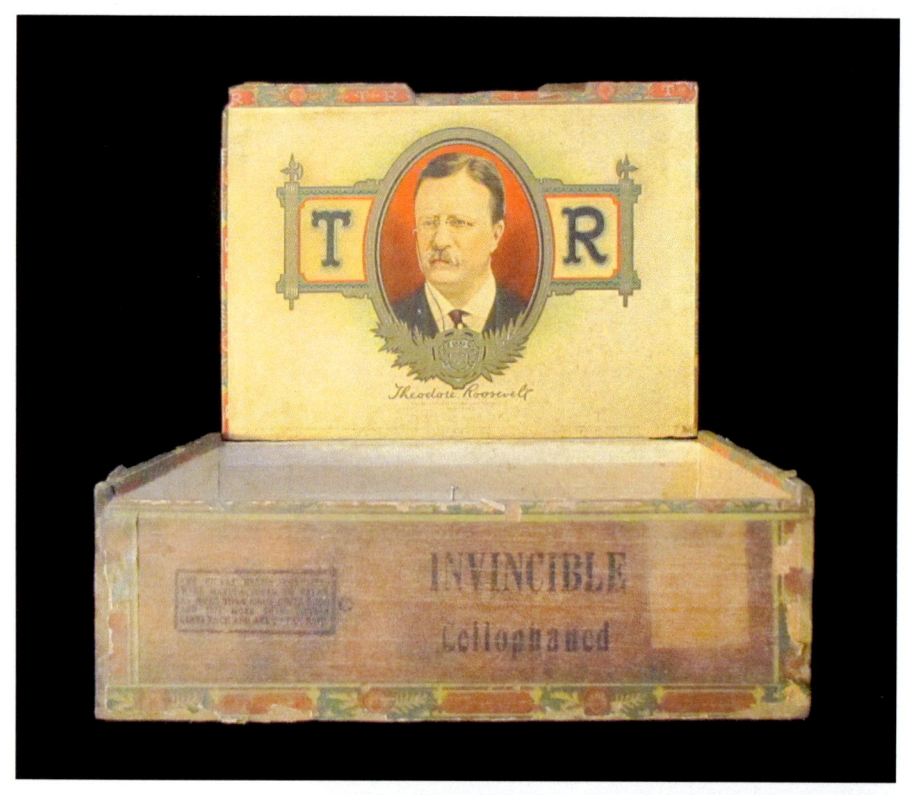

T R cigar box.
Circa 1904.

General Arthur cigar box. Image of Chester Arthur. Circa 1882.

72

Jackknife. "Our Rough Rider President". Opposite side shows view of U.S. Capital. Circa 1904.

Clay pipe. Teddy Roosevelt as Rough Rider. Made In England. Circa 1898.

Our Candidates cigar box label promoting Taft and Sherman. Circa 1908.

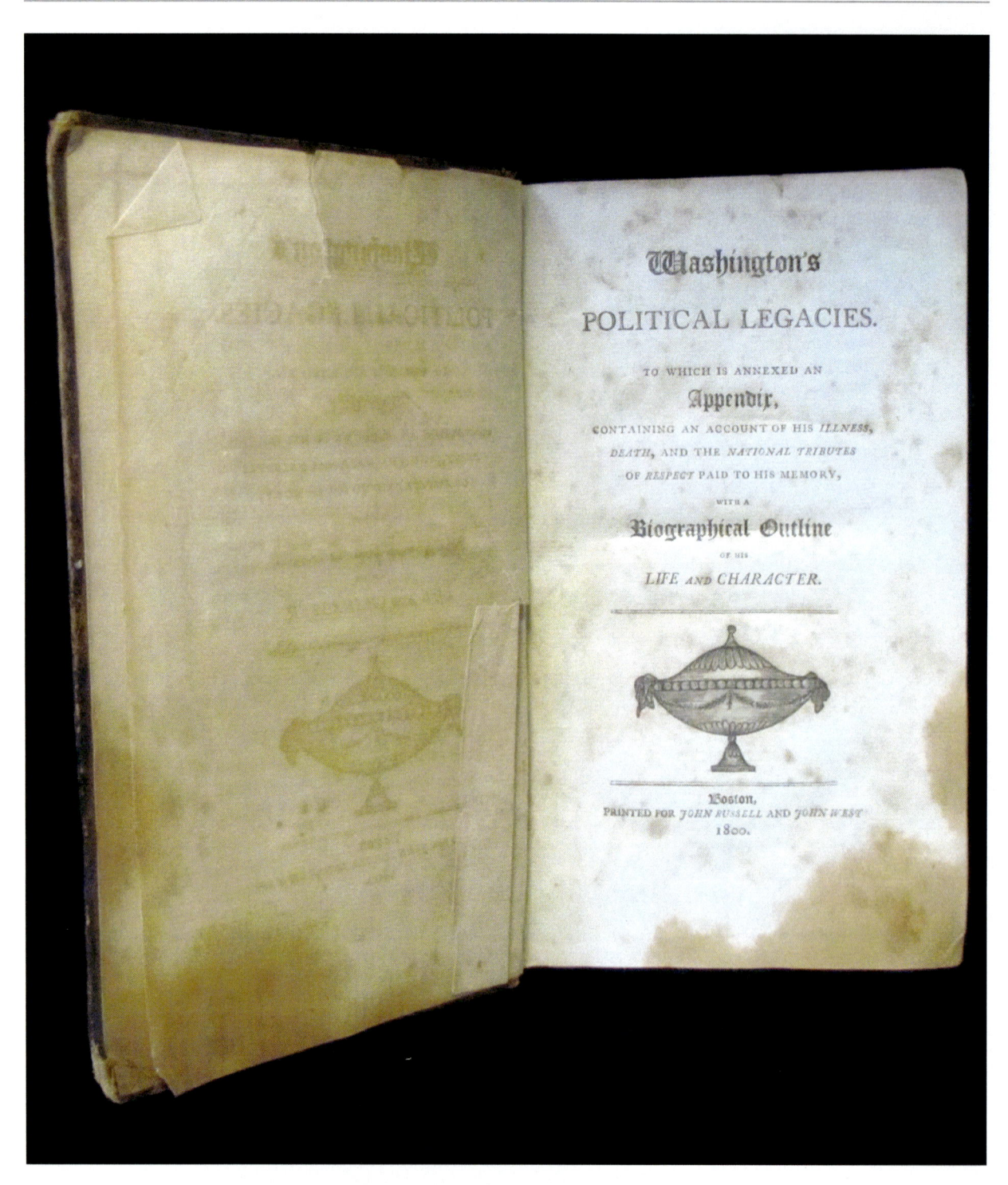

Book. *Washington's Political Legacies.*
Printed in March 1800 shortly after Washington's death.
The introduction is a dedication letter to Mrs. Washington.

Campaign coverlet. W.H. Taft. Circa 1908.
Note: Teddy Roosevelt as Rough Rider on border.

Pewter gift box.
The Inaugural Luncheon
January 20, 2001.
This box was given to
President and Mrs. Carter
when they attended the luncheon
for newly elected George W. Bush.

Campaign lithograph for Franklin Pierce and William King.
Grand, National, Democratic banner by Currier. Hand colored. 1852.

In the House of Representatives, Jan. 19, 1837.

WHEREAS, the term of service of General Andrew Jackson, President of the United States, will expire on the fourth day of March, in the year one thousand eight hundred and thirty-seven; and whereas, the administration of the general government, under the direction and guidance of the President aforesaid, has met, and still does meet the entire approbation and hearty co-operation of a large majority of the people of the United States, and particularly the citizens of the commonwealth of Pennsylvania. And whereas they have hailed, and still do hail with feelings of gratitude and unalterable affection, the *Hero and Statesman* who has nobly and fearlessly defended his country and its liberties in the field and in the cabinet, through a stormy, perilous and eventful life, from BOYHOOD to OLD AGE. And whereas, an irregular and unconstitutional attack was made on the reputation of the people's choice, the President aforesaid, in the Senate of the United States, on the twenty-eighth day of March, in the year one thousand eight hundred and thirty-four; and whereas the public acts and reputation of the patriotic executive of this republic, sustained by the people, are the acts and reputation of the people themselves: and whereas it is the wish, desire and determination of a large majority of the people of this commonwealth that, the name, fame, character and conduct of their veteran President, shall go down to posterity untarnished and unsullied. Therefore,

Resolved by the House of Representatives of the commonwealth of Pennsylvania, That the passage of the resolution by the Senate of the United States, censuring the President of the United States, for a removal of the deposites, was unwise, inexpedient, unconstitutional and unjust, and that the expurgation from the Journal of the Senate of the aforesaid resolution, is in the opinion of this House, a most salutary and constitutional redress for an unconstitutional attack on the character of the President of the United States, and that the Speaker of the House of Representatives be, and he is hereby directed to forward a copy of the foregoing preamble and resolution to the President of the United States, and also one copy to each of the Senators from the state of Pennsylvania, in the Senate of the said United States.

Original Pennsylvania House of Representatives Preamble and Resolution, Jan. 19, 1837, calling for the U.S. senate to expunge the 1834 censure of President Andrew Jackson. Remnants of wax seal and Harrisburg stamp along with a hand written address to Moses Davis Esq. Berwick, PA. on folded reverse side. Also, hand written note at bottom.

Inaugural souvenir mirror.
Dwight D. Eisenhower
January 20, 1953.

Cleveland cabinet card.
Note that it is labeled
S. Grover Cleveland.
Circa 1880

Escort I.D. badge for unknown event involving President Teddy Roosevelt. Circa 1902.
Souvenir cabinet card for a presidential visit. Unknown location, 1902.

Porcelain plates.
Theodore Roosevelt.
Upper plate nine inches.
Lower plate ten inches.
Circa 1903.

Plate.
William H. Taft.
Seven inches.
Circa 1908.

Dish. Five inches.
Shows President Johnson with U.C.P. poster children
at the White House.
1964.

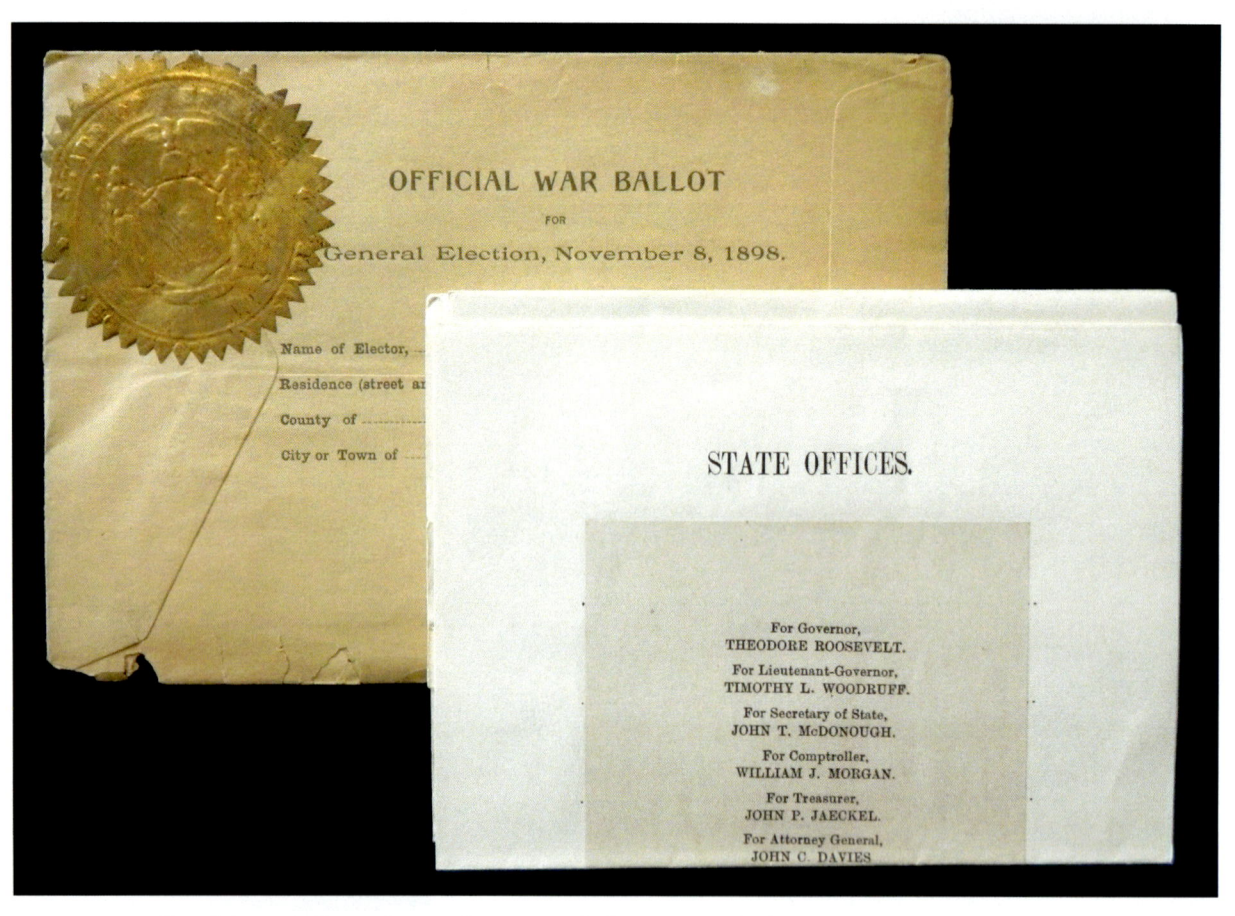

Official War Ballot. State of New York for General Election, November 8, 1898.
Top of ballot lists Theodore Roosevelt for Governor.

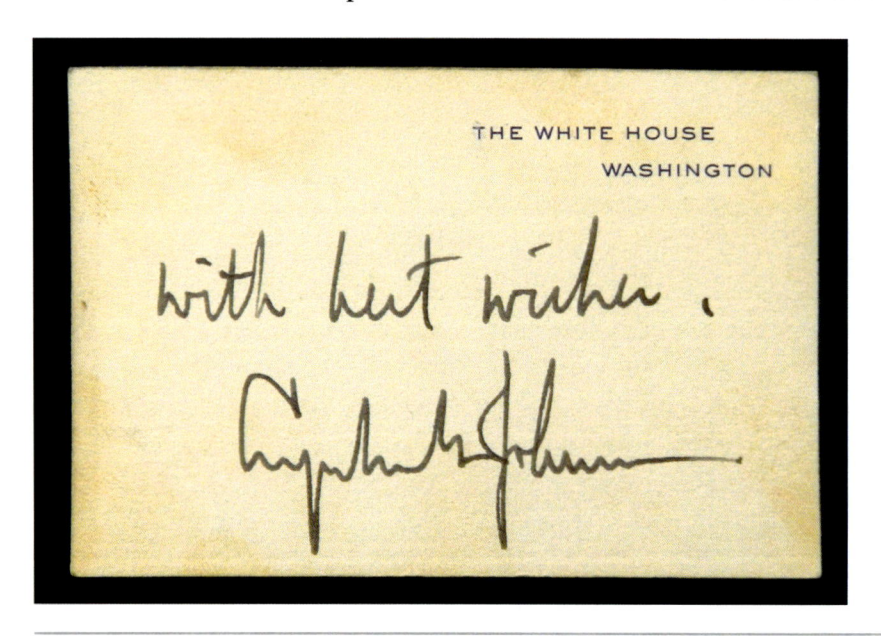

White House card. Hand signed by Lyndon Johnson. Circa 1965.

82

Photo print of President McKinley. Printed at The Pan-American Exposition.
Buffalo, New York 1901.

J.F.K. sculpture. Bronzed pottery on walnut base. Circa 1964.

Copper Plaque.
Commemorating 200th birthday
of George Washington.
Distributed by the
Automobile
Mutual Insurance Company
of America.
1931.

Token. Welcome Home Theodore Roosevelt.
Souvenir of Roosevelt's Return from Africa Hunting Trip.
1910.

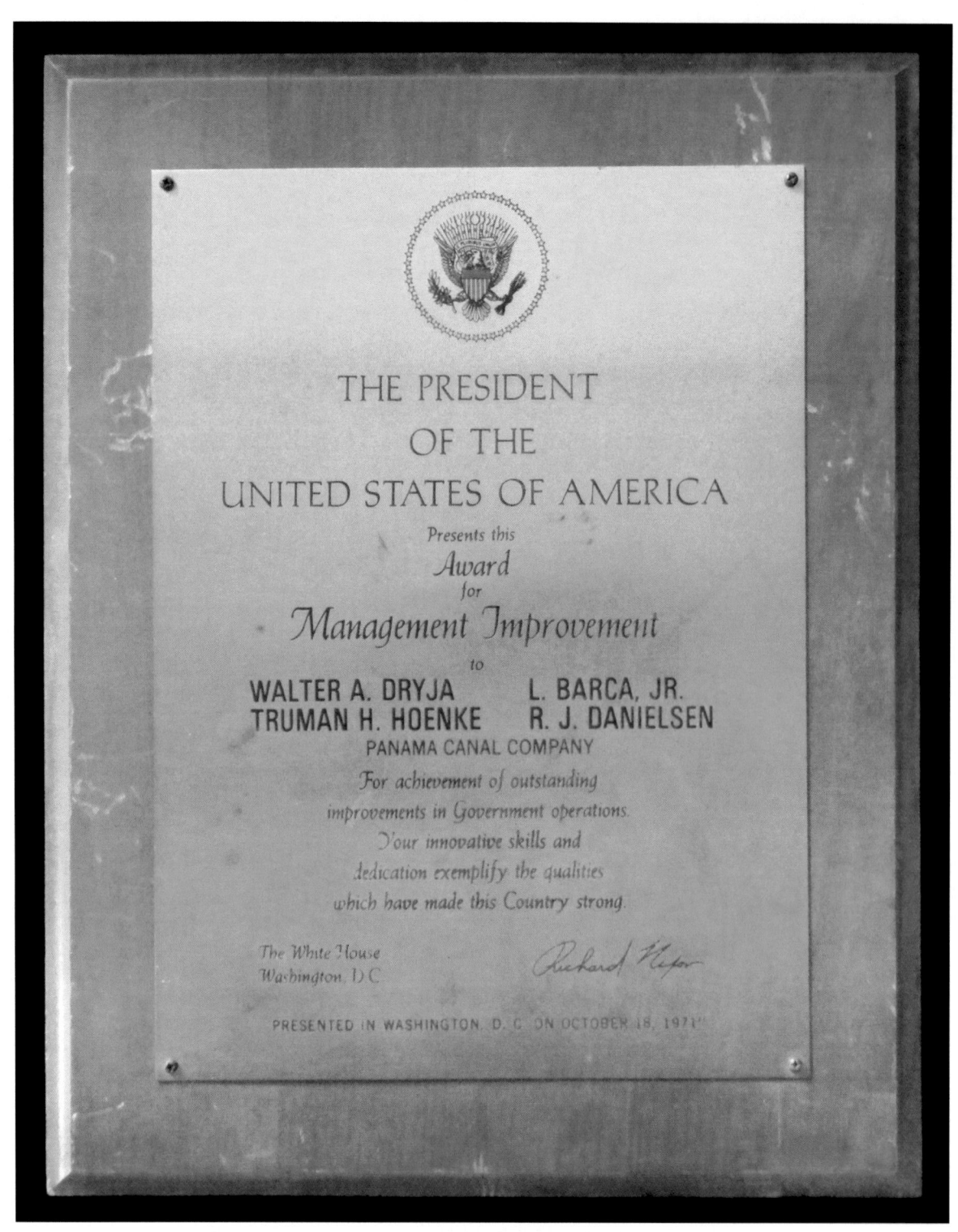

Presidential Award. Engraved metal on wood plaque.
Presented by Richard Nixon to The Panama Canal Company on October 18, 1971.

1904 Republican National Convention. Delegate Badge, Campaign Token and Guest Ticket.

Framed print on canvas. Abraham Lincoln.
Advertising item for The Illinois Watch Company. Circa 1900.

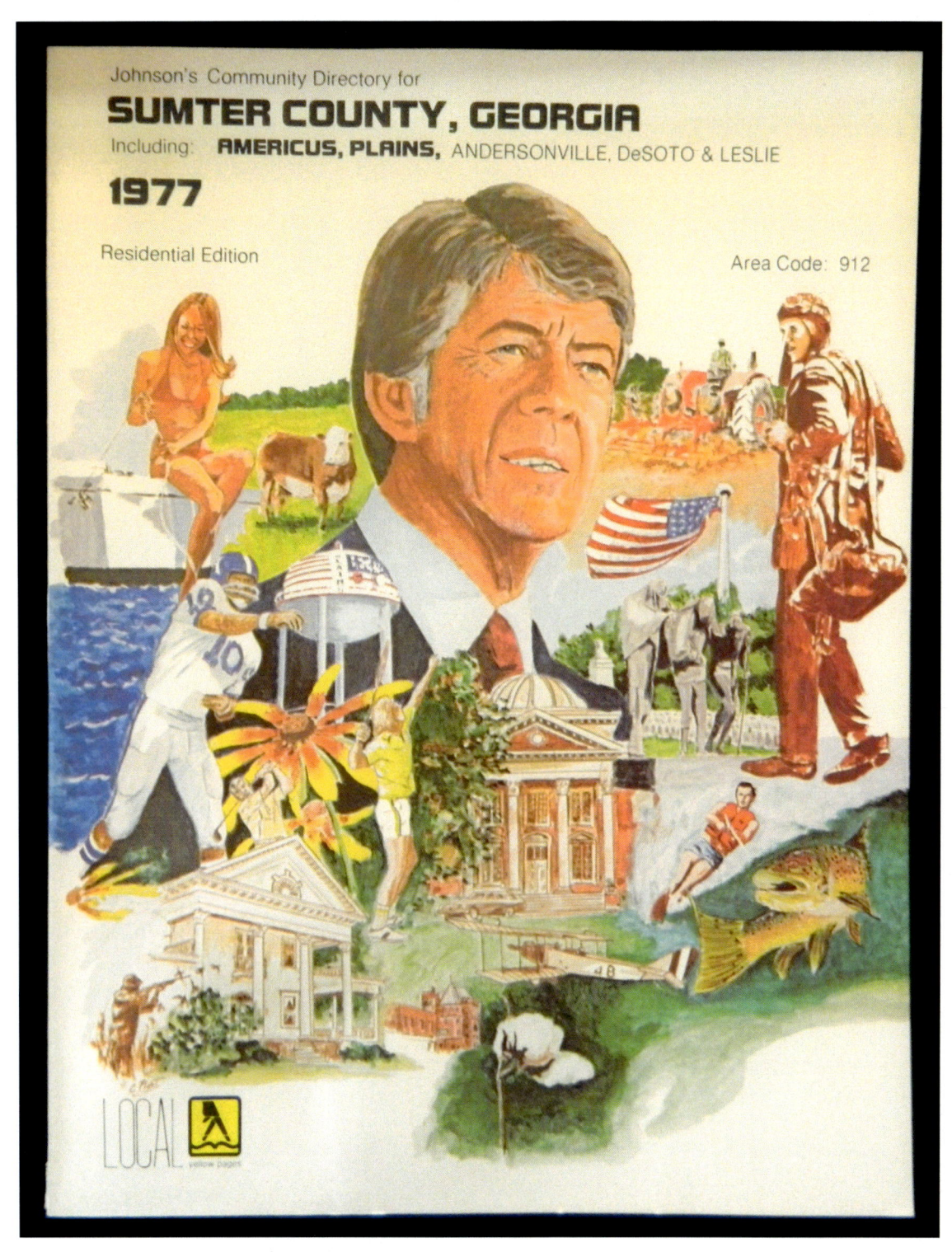

Phone book. Sumter County Georgia. 1977.
The last phone book to list a phone number for Jimmy and Rosalynn Carter.

Four framed Christmas cards. Matted and framed.
Cards are all from Senator and Mrs. John F. Kennedy.
Circa mid to late 1950's.

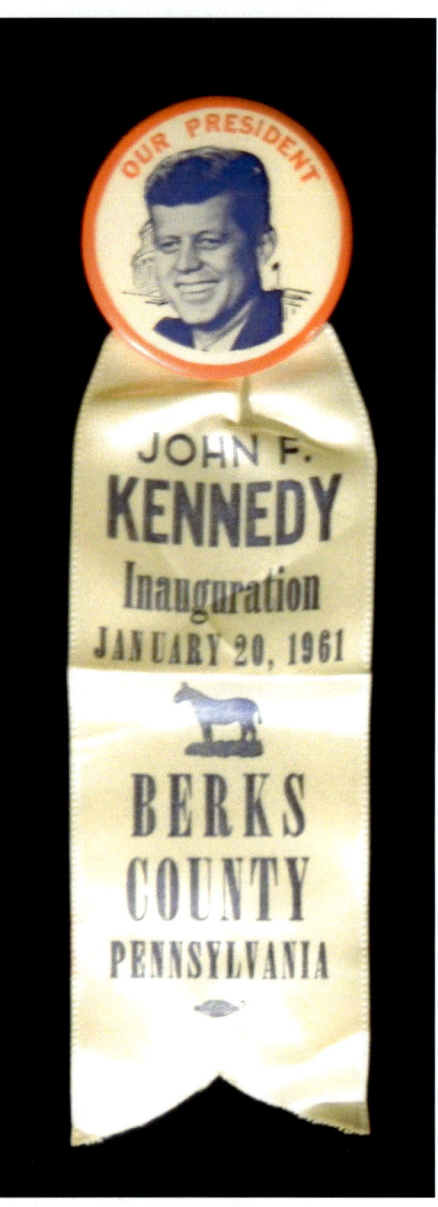

J.F.K. Inauguration pin
and ribbon.
1961.

90

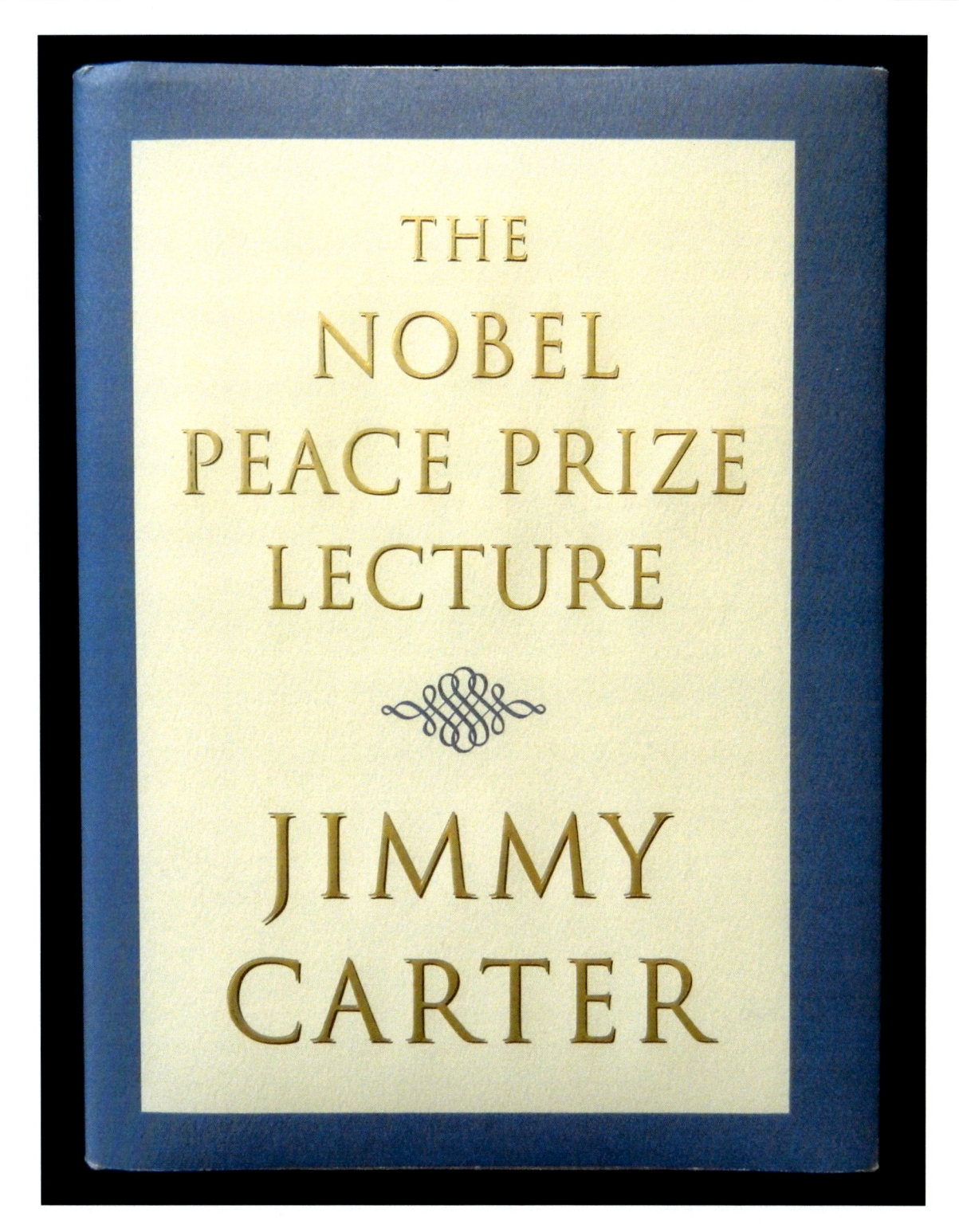

The Nobel Peace Prize Lecture by Jimmy Carter. Hand signed.

Calendar plate.
Nine inch.
Compliments of
Ladies Weekly Journal.
Publishing & Premium Co.
Scranton PA. 1912.

Bowl.
Scene with Lincoln
as a rail splitter.
Circa 1950.

Record.
Excerpts from Richard M. Nixon's
nomination acceptance speech.
Unused. 1968.

Campaign jackknives. 1980 campaign.

National Democratic Convention pin. Houston. 1928.

Pottery bank.
House in which
Abraham Lincoln was born.
Advertising for
Van Dyk Teas.
Circa 1900.

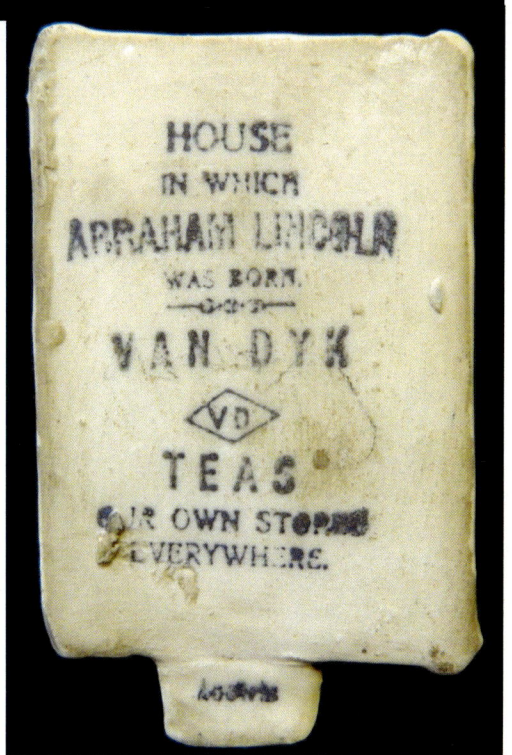

95

E PLURIBUS UNUM.

TELEGRAPH.

HARRISBURG:

Wednesday, March 4, 1840.

Democratic Candidates.

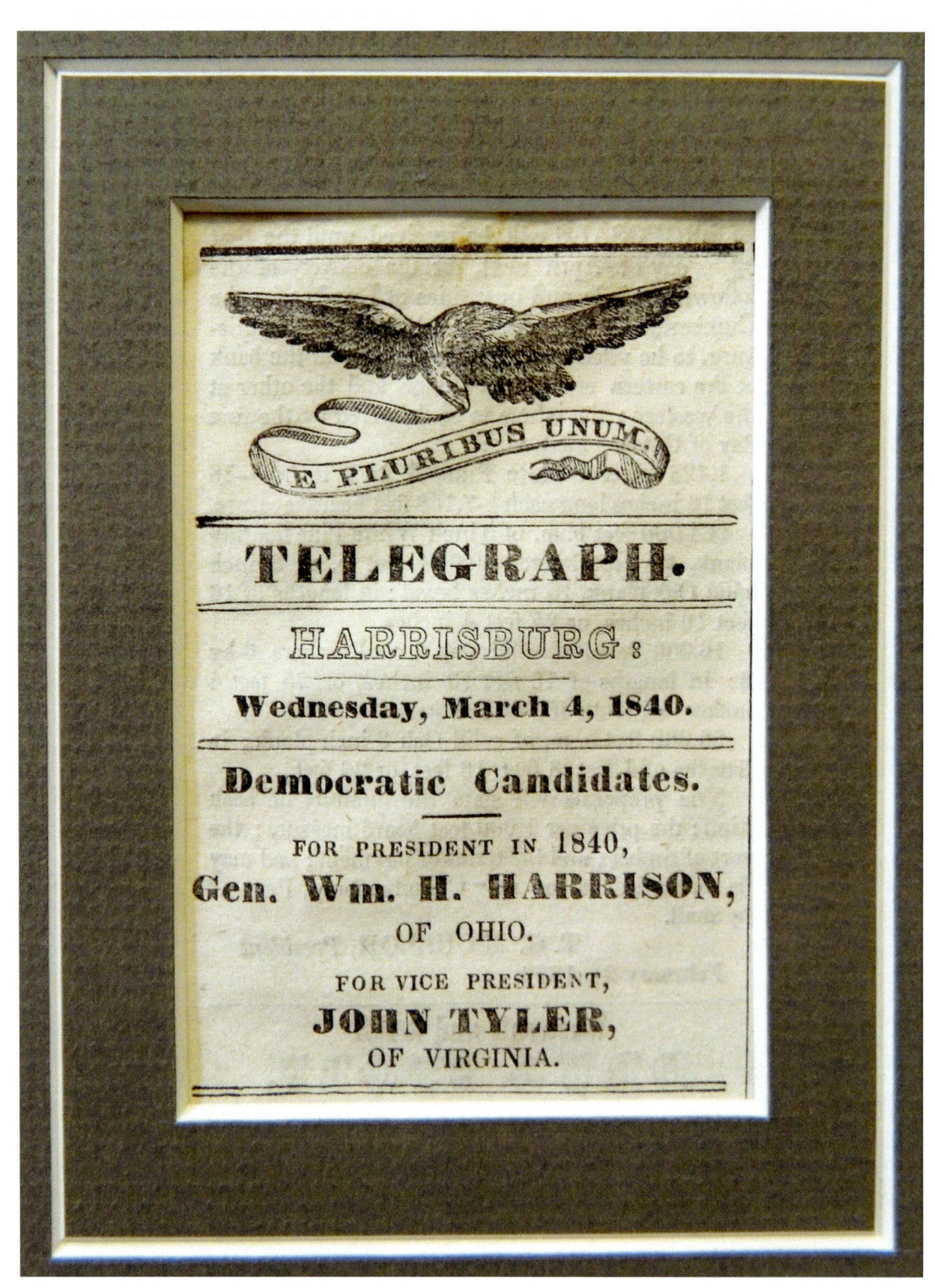

FOR PRESIDENT IN 1840,
Gen. Wm. H. HARRISON,
OF OHIO.

FOR VICE PRESIDENT,
JOHN TYLER,
OF VIRGINIA.

Original newspaper notice. Whig Convention. Harrisburg, PA. 1840.

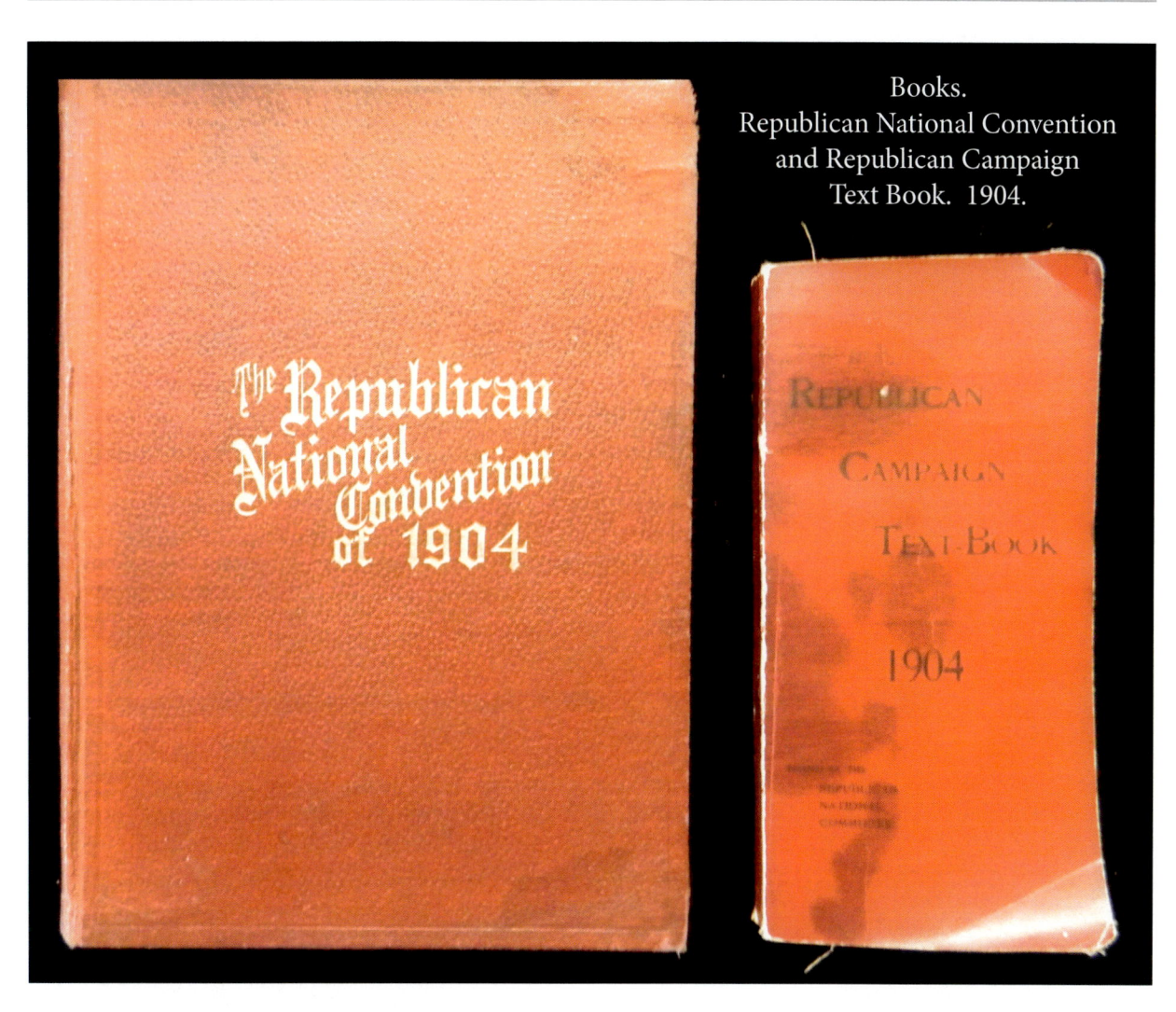

Books.
Republican National Convention and Republican Campaign Text Book. 1904.

George Bush tie clip. Original box. Circa 1990

White House luggage tag.
Circa 1960.

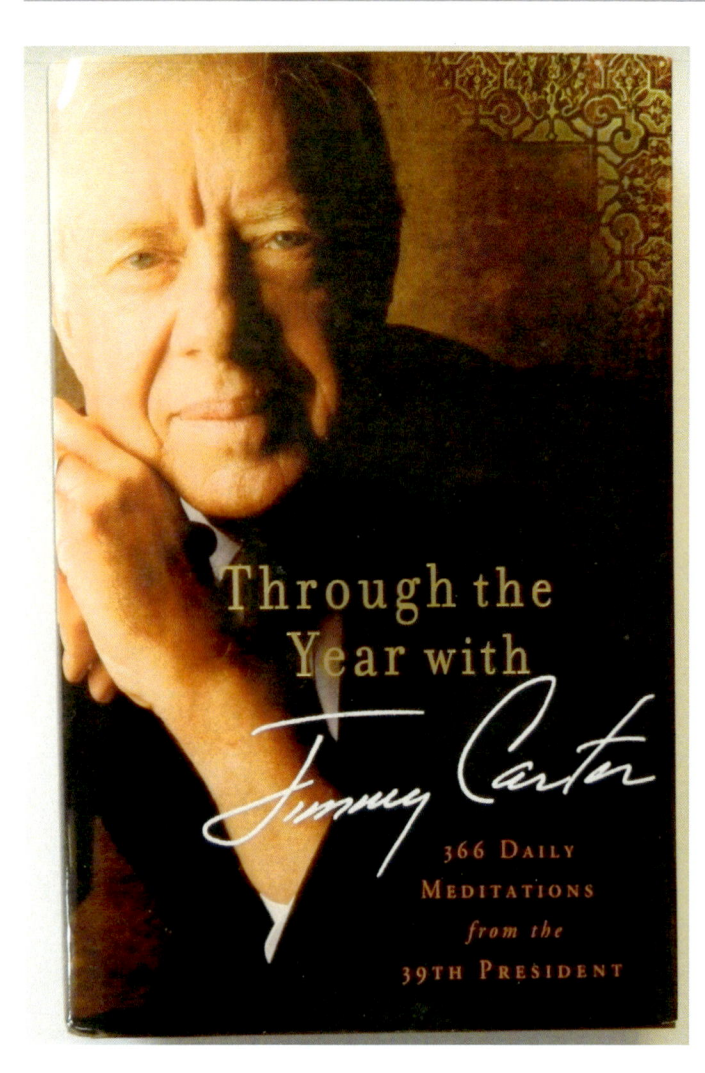

Through the Year with Jimmy Carter by Jimmy Carter. Hand signed. 2011.

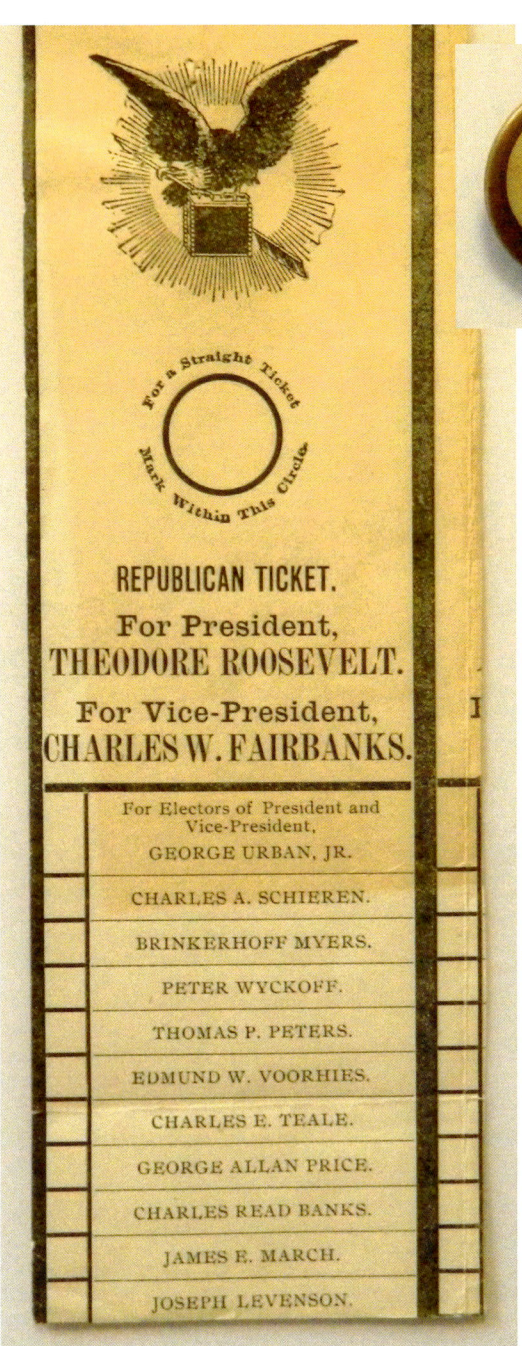

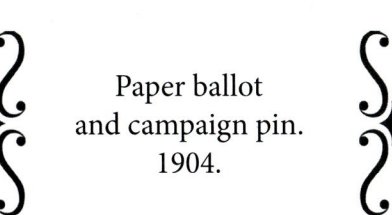

Plastic figure.
J.F.K and John-John.
Titled "Father's Love".

Paper ballot and campaign pin. 1904.

99

EXECUTIVE OFFICE OF THE PRESIDENT OF THE UNITED STATES
OFFICE OF MANAGEMENT AND BUDGET

CONCLUSION

Coincidences and facts discussed in this book have played a part in virtually every administration either directly or indirectly. These events have been influential in forming and changing the presidency throughout American history.

Known as the most powerful office in the world, the presidency has been occupied by men with little or no formal education, educators, laborers and professionals. Some sought the office for years, others were propelled into office rapidly and unexpectedly. Some loved being president, others found it to be lonely and overwhelming. Some lived to be president, others died being president.

All shared the drive, determination and desire to seek and achieve the highest office in the land, forever foregoing personal privacy and securing a permanent place in American history.

Collecting presidential memorabilia is a true testament to the people and events that have made history and shaped a nation.

BIBLIOGRAPHY

Anthony, Carl Sferrazza. *America's First Families.*
New York: Lisa Drew Book/Touchstone Books, Simon & Schuster, 2000.

Bowman, John. *The History of the American Presidency.*
North Dighton Massachusetts: World Publications Group Inc., 1998.

Carter, Jimmy. *White House Diary.* New York: Farrar, Straus and Giroux, 2010.

DeGregorio, William A. *The Complete Book of U.S. Presidents.*
New York: Gramercy Books, 2001.

Freidel, Frank. *Our Country's Presidents.* Washington, D.C.:
National Geographic Society, 1996.

Humes, James. *Which President Killed a Man?* New York: MJF Books, 2003.

Kelly, C. Brian. *Best Little Stories from the White House.* Nashville TN:
Cumberland House, 1999.

Kunhardt, Phillip B. Jr., Kunhardt, Phillip B. III and Kunhardt, Peter W.
The American President. New York: Riverhead Books, 1999.

Rubel, David. *Mr. President The Human Side of America's Chief Executives.*
Alexandria VA.: Time-Life Books, 1998.

Sueling, Barbara. *The Last Cow on the White House Lawn & Other Little Known Facts About the Presidency.* New York: Doubleday & Co., 1978.

Smith, Carter. *Presidents All You Need to Know.* New York: Hylas Publishing, 2005.